FISH AND SHELLFISH

FISH AND SHELLFISH

the essential cookbook   Aldo Zilli

Photography by David Munns

whitecap

First published in North America in 2006 by
Whitecap Books
351 Lynn Avenue
North Vancouver, BC
V7J 2C4

Publisher: Jacqui Small
Managing Editor: Kate John
Design: Janet James
Editor: Anne McDowall
Home Economist: Luisa Alves
Stylist: Roisin Nield
Production: Peter Colley

ISBN 10 – 1-55285-737-9
ISBN 13 – 978-155285-737-3

2006 2007

10 9 8 7 6 5 4 3 2 1

A catalogue record for this book is available from the British Library

Printed in Singapore

Half title:
Marinated anchovies, page 84

Frontispiece:
Oyster tempura, page 140

Above, left to right: Salt cod fish cakes with parsley sauce, page 40; Salmon stuffed with crab and spinach with dill sauce, page 71; Oysters on ice with shallots, red wine vinegar and lemon, page 141

Right: Shrimp soufflé, page 114

CONTENTS

Introduction   6

Round Fish   10
Flat Fish   46
Oily Fish   64
Exotic Fish   92
Shellfish   108

Index   142
Acknowledgments   144

INTRODUCTION

As I start writing, I couldn't be more inspired about fish. I am sitting in one of the best seafood restaurants on the Adriatic coast in the region of Abruzzo, where I was born. I am with ten English people who have bought a weekend course at my cookery school and everybody is very impressed so far. This afternoon we were at Pescara fish market, where fish is auctioned off to restaurateurs and fish stores, and we saw the biggest octopus that I have ever seen in my life – it weighed 110lb!

My love affair with fish started quite early in my life. When I was 11, my dad decided to move from the farm that he had managed with my mum and retire by the sea. My seven brothers, one sister, and I all had to find jobs. I was the youngest and, in my school holidays, I worked for our local fish store – no problems with child labor in those days! At the end of my shift every week I was paid in fish, normally caught on that day – anything from sea bass to monkfish, clams, or mussels. It wasn't until I was a lot older that I appreciated that early apprenticeship in cleaning and gutting fish, but my mum loved my job because it supplied her with enough food to feed all of us. Sunday lunch would normally consist of a nice, fresh, large fish with roasted potatoes and salad.

We also ate a lot of blue fish, such as mackerel and sardines, which are really cheap and very good for you. Since taking part in the UK television show *Celebrity Fit Club*, oily fish has become a mainstay of my diet and I have noticed a big change in my life in general. I look and feel better – my skin is clearer and I now have loads more energy.

If you are buying fish to cook and eat at home, my advice is to venture into a good market, as supermarket fish counters are rarely as good or their fish as fresh. My favorite ones in London have to be Billingsgate Fish Market and Borough Market. Wherever you buy your fish, the best way of telling if it is really fresh is by its smell: a 'fishy' smell is normally an indication that it is quite old. When choosing fish, always look for bright eyes and firm flesh. If the eyes are sunk into the head, this normally means the fish has been dead for more than 48 hours. If you can see blood under the gills, the fish has not been dead for very long.

Ask for the fish to be cleaned but not necessarily filleted. Whether you are cooking sea bass, bream, mackerel, monkfish, Dover sole, or even a very large fish for a dinner party, such as halibut, brill, or turbot, you will find that roasting it whole not only makes a much better centerpiece, but also that most of the flavor comes from the bones.

The best cooking methods for fish are usually the most simple. One of the easiest yet most effective ways to cook a whole fish is to stuff it with rosemary and garlic and roast it with new potatoes, zucchini, onions, small Italian cherry tomatoes, and a whole fresh chili, then add a bit of water. (You can use basil or thyme instead of rosemary if you prefer.) The result will be delicious! There are, of course, many varied cooking methods for fish: one of my other favorites is barbecuing, but fish that has been poached or baked in foil or a banana leaf tastes equally good.

When cooking clams to make for your spaghetti sauce at home, don't add white wine to them: if the clams are fresh, the alcohol will take away a lot of the flavor from them, so just add water. But make sure you invest in a great bottle of extra virgin olive oil to finish off the dish. Indeed, good-quality extra virgin olive oil is an essential store-cupboard ingredient if you're going to cook fresh fish. The oil should be light green in color and the bottle should be nice and dark. You can get a good olive oil for around $18 for 18fl oz. Whatever you do, don't cook with this olive oil though; this is just to finish off your fish dish. Buy a cheaper one for cooking. Other great ingredients for fish are lime, cilantro, ginger, and a little sesame oil, especially if you are marinating a fresh piece of tuna.

At my restaurant in London's Soho, Zilli Fish, the most popular way of eating fish, especially on a Friday, is deep-fried: we sell at least 50 servings of cod and fat fries every Friday lunchtime. Although it is traditional to eat fish on a Friday, many people don't seem to realise that you can eat cod, haddock, or codling in many other ways – it doesn't have to be fried. Personally, I would prefer to eat cod that has been roasted with a little garlic, cherry tomatoes, and olive oil, and, as cod is so expensive nowadays, I feel that cooking it in a deep-fat fryer is a waste. But I won't be taking the British national dish off the menu at Zilli Fish, particularly as it's a best seller! If you do order deep-fried fish and fries in a restaurant, check that the batter is a light golden color. Unfortunately, some chefs don't change the oil in

the fat fryer often enough and it becomes dark in color. The food shouldn't smell of oil and the fries shouldn't smell of fish, as they should be fried in different oil from the fish.

Squid is another victim of the deep-fat fryer; I tried serving it stuffed and grilled but people still prefer it deep-fried. When buying squid, make sure that the body is a nice white color and that it doesn't smell of fish at all. Ask your fish store to clean the squid in front of you so that you can check the color of the body. Squid is one of those fish that is quite difficult to cook. Cook it too little and it is rubbery; cook it too long and it becomes tough. When cooking squid to make a salad, boil it in water with a wine cork as this will make the squid tender. My favorite recipe in the book is the grilled squid with sweet chili sauce (see page 45). Lovely and fresh, especially when served with an arugula and Parmesan salad, it makes a great light lunch!

At my restaurant, people come to eat and be entertained and it is our job to make life easier for our customers by serving fish off the bone or as steaks – tuna, swordfish, or shark. When it comes to eating shellfish – crab, lobster, langoustine, shrimp, clams, and mussels – the fun is in the presentation and in getting stuck in. When you order lobster, first ask the waiter to show it to you alive – it should be a light blue/black color as lobster only turns pink when boiled – and never request it out of the shell. Simply ask for a finger bowl and make as much mess as possible – great fun!

In preparing this book, I was able to experiment with various exotic fish, such as parrot fish and pomfret, and also tried out, for me, some very different recipes, including curries and some Japanese and Chinese dishes. I had great fun and learnt a lot more about all sorts of different fish. I hope this book will inspire you, too, to cook and eat more fish and seafood. Good luck! God bless! Buon Appetito!

Carp

Catfish

Gray mullet

Sea robin

Cod

Gilt-head bream

Sea bass

Perch

Red mullet

Round Fish

Red snapper

Sea bream

Round Fish

This is an extremely large category—including such fish as cod, haddock, hake, ling, whiting, pollock, and mullet, to name just a few—so it would be impossible to include all of them in this book. If you come across another type of round fish that you wish to use instead of the ones I have selected for the recipes in this chapter, try and make sure that the flesh of the fish matches that of the fish I have chosen.

Round fish have an eye on either side of their head; many of their bones are attached to their fins and all will contain small pin bones. Of all the round fish, sea bass is probably the most well known. It has wonderful skin that becomes lovely and crispy when grilled or pan-fried; do eat the skin as it adds to the flavor of this fish. Most round fish have white, delicate flesh, which makes them fantastic fish to roast whole with a little rosemary, garlic, and lemon. Round fish are the most well known of all fish and so you are likely to have at least a general understanding of most of the fish that are featured in this chapter.

BLACK COD *Anoplopoma fimbria*
This marine fish, also known as the small scaled cod, can grow to 14 inches and weigh as much as 6lb 10oz. It is not related to true cod, but is extremely good to eat.

BREAM
Most of the varieties of bream have a juicy, dense, white flesh. Most commonly available is the red sea bream (genera *Pagellus* and *Spondyliosoma*), but the gilt-head bream (*Sparus aurata*) is considered the best of all and has juicy white flesh. It is now being farmed.

CARP *Cyprinus carpio*
These hardy fish live in lakes, ponds, and slow-moving rivers, which makes them a good fish to farm. They have meaty flesh and grow to about 20 inches and weigh around 6lb 10oz. The scales can be quite large; pour boiling water over to dislodge them.

CATFISH
Catfish are the fifth most consumed fish in the USA. Most catfish are freshwater varieties (*Ictalurus*). It is firm, low in fat, and farmed catfish has a mild flavour. Remove the tough skin from the fish before cooking.

COD *Gadus morhua*
Cod used to be considered a cheap option, but it has been over fished and is now relatively scarce and a lot more expensive. It is a succulent fish with white flaky flesh and lends itself to most cooking methods.

HADDOCK *Melanogrammus aeglefinus*
Part of the cod family, haddock are generally smaller than cod but can be used in the same way. Haddock is especially popular when smoked.

JOHN DORY *Zeus faber*
This fish is easily recognizable by the thumb prints on the sides of its body. It has a huge head, which, along with fins and bones, accounts for about 60 percent of its weight.

MONKFISH *Lophius piscatorius*
This very ugly fish is almost always sold without its enormous head. It is the tail that is eaten and this has a firm, white flesh and no little bones.

MULLET
The gray mullet (*Liza auratus*) resembles sea bass but has larger scales and a smaller mouth. It lives near the sea bed, so may smell muddy. If so, soak it in water and

vinegar, changing this often. Red mullet (*Mullus surmuletus*) are smaller and have a rich taste and firm flesh.

PERCH
There are two varieties: freshwater perch (*Perca fluviatilis*) and ocean perch (*Sebastes marinus*). In season they are good pan-fried; out of season use them in stews or soups.

POLLOCK *Pollachius virens*
Also called the saithe, coalfish, or coley, pollock is a less well-known member of the cod family that has the same advantages as cod – firm, white, fleshy meat and almost no fat content. Lots of fried fish restaurants sell this and it is an extremely good alternative to both cod, which is becoming increasingly expensive, and haddock.

RED SNAPPER *Lutjanus campechanis*
Found all over the world, this fish is in high demand, which has led to a high price. Red snapper has a firm texture and an almost nutty flavor. When buying look for clear, red eyes and bright red skin that fades toward the belly. Buy fillets with the skin on to help retain the flavor of the fish.

Snappers are available all year round and are fantastic for grilling whole.

SEA BASS genus *Centropristus*
One the finest fish available with firm flesh, a delicate flavor and only a few small bones. Most sea bass is now farmed, but wild, line-caught fish have the best flavor. The skin of sea bass is excellent to eat but make sure you remove all the tough scales.

SEA ROBIN genus *Friglidae*
Sea robins have a relatively large bony plated head and narrow body with lots of spines. These are very sharp so be careful when cleaning. They tend to be quite cheap and are normally sold whole.

SHAD genus *Alosa*
Well known to fish sportsmen, shad have many bones but a delicate flavor. Long or slow cooking can soften small bones enough to make them edible.

SQUID genus *Loligo*
These marine molluscs are found worldwide and there are numerous species. Squid are sold fresh, whole, or cleaned and sliced, or frozen. They should not smell of fish: "fishy" squid is old and will be tough. To soften, leave in a bowl of milk.

Grilled red mullet with bay leaves

When buying red mullet make sure the skin is a nice red color and is not marked or broken. When you press down on the skin, the flesh should feel firm and not soft. This is a good fish for the barbecue or for roasting whole.

SERVES: 4

Preparation time: 5 minutes
Cooking time: 25 minutes

4 whole red mullet (14oz each),
   scaled and cleaned
4 garlic cloves, crushed
4 sprigs rosemary
4 sprigs thyme
¼ cup olive oil
sea salt
2 garlic cloves, finely chopped
1 red chili, seeded and finely
   chopped
1 Tbsp lemon juice
¼ cup finely chopped parsley
36 bay leaves
steamed spinach or bok choy
   to serve

method

1 Stuff each mullet with a quarter of the crushed garlic, a sprig of rosemary, and a sprig of thyme, brush with olive oil and sprinkle over some sea salt.

2 Heat the remaining olive oil and cook the chopped garlic and chili for about 5 minutes. Remove from the heat and strain. Allow to cool, then whisk in the lemon juice and parsley.

3 Brush a barbecue with olive oil, then place the bay leaves on top to form a bed for the fish. Cook the mullet on top of the bay leaves for 10 minutes, then carefully turn them over and cook for a further 10 minutes.

4 Serve the fish on top of some steamed spinach or bok choy. Warm through the dressing and pour it over the fish.

Alternative fish:
bream, grayling, snapper

1 Using a pair of scissors, cut into the belly of the fish near the tail. Cut toward the head to make a long slash.

2 Reach into the belly, grab hold of the intestines, and pull them out. Wash the inside of the fish thoroughly under cold water.

3 Using a pair of scissors, cut off all the fins.

4 Holding the tail firmly, descale the fish. Push the knife away from you and toward the head. Be careful not to cut into the flesh.

Thai roast sea bass

I love Thai cooking at the moment. Lots of dishes on my menu use Asian herbs and spices and they accompany sea bass particularly well. I was inspired to make this recipe after one of my trips to my local Thai restaurant last year; now I cook it at home.

SERVES: 4

Preparation time: 10 minutes plus 1 hour marinating time
Cooking time: 20 minutes

2lb whole sea bass, scaled and gutted, head on
1 garlic clove, thinly sliced
2 tsp soy sauce
2 Tbsp good dry white wine
1 Tbsp extra virgin olive oil
1 red chili, seeded and finely chopped
½-inch piece fresh gingerroot, finely chopped
1 Tbsp roughly chopped cilantro
arugula and Parmesan salad to serve (optional)

method

1 Cut 3 diagonal slices in the body of the fish and place it on a marinating tray. Push the sliced garlic into each slit. Mix together the soy sauce, white wine, and olive oil and stir in the chopped chili, ginger, and cilantro. Pour evenly all over the fish and leave to marinate for 1 hour. Preheat the oven to 425°F.

2 Place a large piece of aluminum foil in a roasting pan large enough to hold the fish. Lay the fish in the center and lift up the sides of the foil. Pour the marinade all over the fish then pinch together the edges of the foil to make a parcel.

3 Cook in the oven for 20 minutes. Remove from the oven and place the whole parcel in a large serving platter. Open the foil and serve at the table, with an arugula and Parmesan salad if desired.

Alternative fish:
gray mullet, red snapper, bream

Right: Thai roast sea bass

Sesame baked red snapper

This is another favorite method of cooking fish; wrapping the fish helps it to retain flavor and the presentation is fantastic. I found this dish in a restaurant in Barbados where Nikki and I got married, so it has lots of memories for me.

SERVES: 4

Preparation time: 10 minutes plus
   4–5 hours marinating time
Cooking time: 35 minutes

2 Tbsp vegetable oil
2 tsp sesame oil
2 tsp sesame seeds
1-inch piece fresh gingerroot, very
   thinly sliced
2 garlic cloves, crushed
2 small red chilies, seeded and
   finely chopped
1 medium onion, sliced
2 Tbsp white wine
1 Tbsp nam pla (fish sauce)
2 tsp caster sugar
½ tsp cracked pepper
juice of 2 limes
2–4 banana leaves (optional)
2 whole red snapper (400g/
   14oz each)

Stir-fried vegetables
1 Tbsp olive oil
1 garlic clove, crushed
2 red bell peppers, cut into strips
2 yellow bell peppers, cut into
   strips
1 red onion, cut into strips
2 zucchini, cut into strips

Mango crisps
vegetable oil for deep-frying
1 mango, skin left on, sliced thinly
flour for dusting

method

1 To make the marinade, heat the vegetable oil and sesame oil in a wok or pan, add the sesame seeds, and fry until golden. Add the ginger, garlic, chili, and onion and cook over a low heat. Stir in the wine, nam pla, sugar, pepper, and lime juice. Simmer for about 2–3 minutes and then remove from heat, set aside to cool.

2 If you are using banana leaves, make sure to soften the central stem by dipping it in boiling water then rubbing it with vegetable oil to keep the leaf flexible. Banana leaves are inedible, but they will flavor the fish. Alternatively you can use aluminum foil.

3 Spread the marinade over the fish and then wrap them in banana leaves. Thread the leaves with bamboo skewers to keep the leaf together. Place in the refrigerator or another cool place and leave to marinate for 4–5 hours. If using foil roll the edges to form a parcel.

4 Preheat the oven to 350°F. Place the fish parcels on a baking sheet and cook for 35 minutes. (Allow a longer cooking time if your fish are larger than 14oz.)

5 Meanwhile, make the mango crisps. Heat the vegetable oil in a skillet, dust the mango slices with flour, and deep-fry until light golden. Drain on some paper towels and keep warm.

6 A few minutes before the fish is cooked, stir-fry the vegetables. Heat the olive oil, add the garlic to the pan, and cook for 1 minute. Remove the garlic from the pan, then add the red and yellow pepper, red onion, and zucchini and stir-fry for 3 minutes.

7 Remove the fish from the oven and carefully open the parcels. Serve in the middle of the table with the stir-fried vegetables and mango crisps.

Alternative fish:
mullet, grayling, snapper, parrot
fish, monkfish tails

Bream stuffed with thyme and pan-fried in lemon oil

I grew up near the Adriatic Sea and at home we always cooked with whole fish as my mother used to say that the bones gave the fish more flavor. To this day it is still one of my favorite ways of cooking fish.

SERVES: 4

Preparation time: 10 minutes
Cooking time: 25 minutes

3 Tbsp chopped dill
2 Tbsp chopped rosemary
¼ cup chopped parsley
2 tsp chopped thyme
½ tsp salt
½ tsp ground black pepper
2 small whole bream (1lb 2oz each)
2 lemons, sliced
½ cup extra virgin olive oil
6 Tbsp lemon juice
¼ cup white wine

method

1 Preheat the oven to 350°F. Mix the chopped dill, rosemary, parsley, thyme, salt, and pepper and fill each cavity with a slice of lemon and this herb mixture.

2 Heat the oil in a skillet and pan-fry the fish for 5 minutes on each side. Add the lemon juice to the pan and cook for a further 3 minutes on each side.

3 Place the fish on a roasting pan in the oven and bake for 9 minutes.

4 Remove the fish to a plate and then add the white wine to the pan to deglaze. Pour the sauce over the fish and serve immediately with some extra lemon slices.

Alternative fish:
sea bass, grayling

Shad stuffed with sorrel and served with beurre blanc

Sorrel is half vegetable and half herb with a strong, very lemony flavor that marries well with fish. Basil and cherry tomatoes in season make a great salad to serve with any fish and one that complements this dish beautifully.

SERVES: 4

Preparation time: 10 minutes
Cooking time: 20 minutes

4 whole shad (9oz each) or 4 shad
    fillets (6oz each)
2 Tbsp chopped fresh sorrel
2 garlic cloves, finely chopped
2 Tbsp olive oil

Sauce
3 shallots, finely diced
⅓ cup white wine
⅓ cup white wine vinegar
½ cup unsalted butter, diced and
    chilled
1 tsp lemon juice
salt and freshly ground black pepper

method

1 Preheat the oven to 375°F. If you are using whole fish, stuff the cavity of each with a mixture of sorrel and garlic. If using fillets, place a mixture of garlic and sorrel in the middle of each fillet and roll, securing each with a toothpick.

2 Place the whole fish or rolled fillets onto a greased baking sheet and pour the olive oil all over the fish. Bake in the oven for 20 minutes (for whole fish, or 15 minutes if using fish fillets).

3 Meanwhile, make the sauce: simmer the shallots, wine, and vinegar in a saucepan until reduced to about 3 tablespoons of liquid. Remove and set aside to cool for at least 15 minutes.

4 Whisk in the butter, adding it slowly, making sure the butter is completely incorporated before adding any more, to make a pale sauce. Add the lemon juice and season to taste. Leave until ready to be gently reheated to add to the fish.

5 Remove the fish from the oven and pour the hot sauce over.

Alternative fish:
mullet, salmon

*Right: Shad stuffed with sorrel and
served with beurre blanc*

STUFFING A WHOLE FISH

1 Lay the cleaned fish on a board and lift up one side to create an opening. Stuff with lemon and herbs, making sure to fill all the cavity.

FILLETING ROUND FISH

1 Using scissors, snip the fins off the fish. Lift one side of the fish and with a sharp knife trim the fat from the belly, working from head to tail.

2 Turn the fish over and remove the fat from the other side in the same way. Discard the fat.

3 Open out the fish with the skin side up. Using the knife, cut the flesh away from the back bone, working down toward the tail.

4 Turn the fish over and cut the fillet away from the fish. Repeat steps 3 and 4 on the other side to remove the second fillet.

Baked cod with black olive crust and lentils

I first came up with this recipe when I took part in the UK TV show *Celebrity Fit Club*; it helped me to lose weight as it is low in calories and has good nutritional value with iron and lots of protein.

SERVES: 4

Preparation time: 15 minutes
Cooking time: 40 minutes

¼ cup extra virgin olive oil
1 carrot, diced
1 stalk celery, diced
1 onion, chopped
3 cups lentils, soaked overnight if dried
2 bay leaves
1½ quarts vegetable stock
1 Tbsp breadcrumbs
1 tsp each rosemary and thyme
1 cup pitted black olives
4 cod fillets (6oz each)

method

1 Heat half the oil in a large pan and add the carrot, celery, and onion. Cook until soft, about 3–4 minutes, stirring to ensure they don't stick.

2 Add the lentils and bay leaves, stir a couple of times, and then add the stock and cook until it has been absorbed by the lentils, about 30 minutes. Preheat the oven to 350°F.

3 Meanwhile, in a food processor, blend the remaining oil, the breadcrumbs, rosemary, thyme, and black olives until you have a smooth mix.

4 Place the cod fillets in a roasting pan and divide the olive mixture between them. Press down with your fingers and ensure it covers the fillets. Bake in the oven for 7–8 minutes. Serve fish on a bed of lentils.

Alternative fish:
mackerel, salmon, John Dory, halibut

Pan-fried perch with béarnaise sauce

Normally you associate this sauce with a good steak so a good alternative to perch would be tuna. If you use tuna for this recipe, make sure the pan is smoking hot before you add the tuna and then only sear it.

SERVES: 4

Preparation time: 10 minutes
Cooking time: 20 minutes

4 perch fillets (6½oz each)
1 Tbsp olive oil

Sauce
2oz shallots, minced
½ cup tarragon wine vinegar
3 Tbsp finely chopped fresh tarragon
pinch of cracked black peppercorns
6 egg yolks
2½ cups clarified butter, hot
salt to taste
cayenne pepper to taste
fresh lemon juice to taste

method

1 To make the béarnaise sauce, mix together shallots, vinegar, 2 tablespoons tarragon, and peppercorns in a stainless steel pan and simmer until reduced by two thirds. Remove from heat and set aside to cool for 15 minutes.

2 Transfer to a heat-resistant bowl, add the egg yolks, and whisk well. Place the bowl over a pan of simmering water and continue to whisk the sauce until thick and creamy. Be careful that the eggs do not scramble; remove the bowl from heat if you think this is happening.

3 Remove the sauce from the heat and, continuing to whisk, gradually add the hot clarified butter. If the sauce becomes too thick then thin with a little lemon juice or water. Strain the sauce through cheesecloth and season to taste with salt, cayenne pepper, and lemon juice. Add the remaining tarragon.

4 Pan-fry the perch fillets in olive oil for 8 minutes on each side. Reheat the béarnaise sauce and serve with the fish.

Alternative fish:
tuna, monkfish

Left: Baked cod with black olive crust and lentils

FILLETING JOHN DORY

1 Lay the fish on a board and snip off the spiny fins with a pair of scissors.

2 Lifting the gill fin, make a diagonal cut to the top of the head behind the fin.

3 Insert the knife halfway down the backbone, keeping as close to the bone as possible, and cut toward the tail.

4 Keeping the knife flat, continue to cut round the fish until you have separated the entire fillet.

John Dory with tapenade, mash, and spinach

John Dory are easily distinguished from other similar fish by a black spot known as 'St Peter's Thumb'. The story goes that St Peter picked up this fish and left this black mark on its body. It is a great tasting fish and works really well with these ingredients. To serve, arrange the mash, spinach, and fish fillet on each plate in a little tower.

SERVES: 4

Cooking time: 15 minutes
Preparation time: 20 minutes

4 John Dory fillets (8oz each)
6 Tbsp olive oil
3 Tbsp unsalted butter
1 Tbsp lemon juice
1 glass dry white wine
1lb potatoes, peeled and quartered
2lb 10oz spinach, washed and
   tough stalks removed
2 garlic cloves, peeled and crushed
1 fresh red chili, seeded and finely
   chopped
salt and freshly ground black pepper
milk (as necessary for mash)
extra virgin olive oil to serve

Alternative fish:
skate, snapper

Tapenade
1 cup pitted black olives
1 garlic clove, peeled and chopped
1oz fresh anchovy fillets, drained
2 Tbsp capers
squeeze lemon juice
3 fresh basil leaves
1 Tbsp olive oil
freshly ground black pepper

method

1 Make the tapenade first. Place all the ingredients in a food processor and blitz until all are roughly chopped and combined. Set aside for the flavors to infuse.

2 Pan-fry the fillets skin side down in 3 tablespoons of olive oil and 2 tablespoons of the butter for 3 minutes. Add the lemon juice and wine and cook for a further 2 minutes. Turn over the fillets and sauté on the other side for a further 5 minutes. If the pan is getting too dry, add a little more olive oil and lemon juice.

3 Boil the potatoes for 10 minutes until soft enough to mash.

4 Meanwhile, place the spinach leaves in a large heavy-based saucepan (do not add water). Cover the pan and cook gently for 6–7 minutes until the spinach wilts, stirring occasionally to prevent it from sticking to the pan. Drain well and allow to cool slightly, then squeeze out excess water. Chop roughly.

5 Heat 3 tablespoons of oil in the same pan. Stir in the garlic and chili and fry for 2 minutes. Add the spinach, season to taste, and cook until the spinach is heated through.

6 Mash potatoes with remaining butter and milk and season to taste. To serve, place the mash on each plate, top with the spinach, then place a fillet in the center of each. Spoon over the tapenade and drizzle with extra virgin olive oil.

5 Lift up the fillet and carefully slide the knife along the bone to release it completely.

6 Be careful of any pin bones that may remain in the fillet. You will need to remove these with tweezers.

7 The fillet will come away in one piece. Turn the fish over and repeat steps 2–6 on the other side.

8 Tidy up each fillet and cut into pieces as required. The fillets will not be equal in size and shape, but this is normal.

1 Lay 3 strips of Parma ham or bacon side by side on a board. Place the fillet and any other fillings across the Parma ham strips at one end.

2 Lift up the ends of the Parma ham, lay them over the top of the fillings, and pat down. Pull toward you and roll tightly at the same time.

3 Continue rolling tightly until you reach the end. Lay the wrapped fillet on a board with ends underneath until ready to cook.

Monkfish wrapped in Parma ham

Bacon is a good alternative to Parma ham. If you can't find monkfish fillets make sure that the fish you choose instead has suitably firm flesh.

SERVES: 4–6

Preparation time: 20 minutes
Cooking time: 20 minutes

½ small red bell pepper
½ small green bell pepper
½ small yellow bell pepper
2 monkfish fillets (12oz) each
4½oz Parma ham, thinly sliced
1 large sprig rosemary, separated into small sprigs
¼ cup extra virgin olive oil
sliced red onions and tomatoes

Sauce
¾ cup Champagne
3 Tbsp fruit vinegar
½ cup fish stock
3 tsp caster sugar
¼ cup fresh mint leaves, finely chopped
2 Tbsp unsalted butter

Alternative fish:
Dover sole, turbot

method

1 Preheat the oven to 400°F. Cut away the membranes from the peppers, then slice the peppers very finely into strips. Season the monkfish all over.

2 Lay the Parma ham out flat on a work surface with each slice slightly overlapping, then arrange half of the peppers along the center. Place the monkfish fillets on top and lay the remaining pepper slices and half of the rosemary sprigs on the fish. Tightly roll the Parma ham around the monkfish, then pierce the rolls with the remaining rosemary sprigs to secure them.

3 Heat a large heavy-based oven-proof skillet until hot, add the olive oil, and heat until hot. Add the monkfish and seal for 5 minutes, turning the fish constantly.

4 Transfer the pan to the oven and roast for 10 minutes, then turn off the oven and open the door slightly; this will keep the fish warm while you are making the sauce.

5 To make the sauce; place the Champagne in a pan over medium heat and simmer for 6 minutes, then add the vinegar, stock, sugar, and half the mint. Simmer until the liquid is reduced by half. Over a low heat, whisk in the butter, then stir in the remaining mint.

6 Serve the fish on top of sliced red onions and tomatoes with the sauce on the side.

Tahini baked haddock

Again this is quite a healthy recipe; I cook it at home often and Nikki loves it. This dish is great served with some organic hummus and arugula. Don't be afraid to try this recipe—it is incredibly simple and tasty.

SERVES: 4

Preparation time: 10 minutes
Cooking time: 35 minutes

4 haddock fillets (10oz each)
juice of 2 lemons
2 Tbsp extra virgin olive oil
1 cup tahini
1 garlic clove, finely chopped
¼ cup water
2 white onions, sliced
couscous or rice and a herb salad
   to serve (optional)

method

1 Preheat the oven to 400°F. Place a sheet of aluminum foil on the base of a baking sheet or dish and place the haddock fillets on top of the foil. Mix together 1 tablespoon of lemon juice and 1 tablespoon of olive oil and pour the mixture over the fish. Place another piece of foil over the fish and seal the edges to form a parcel. Bake for 15 minutes.

2 Meanwhile mix together the tahini and garlic. In another bowl, combine the remaining lemon juice and the water. Slowly add the lemon juice mix to the tahini, then beat with a whisk until smooth and creamy. Season with salt and freshly ground black pepper to taste.

3 Pan-fry the onions in the remaining olive oil until brown and almost crispy.

4 Remove the fish from the oven and pull off the top layer of foil. Place the onions around the fish and then pour over the tahini mixture and bake for a further 15 minutes, or until the topping is bubbling and a lovely golden color. (Do not replace the foil as you want the fish to start browning.) Serve with some couscous or rice and a herb salad if desired.

Alternative fish:
cod, pollock, John Dory,
codling

Cod in teriyaki and mango

Teriyaki is my new favorite flavor for food, especially with fish. If you choose to use black cod it is quite difficult to find fresh, so buy it frozen. It is one of the few fish that I don't mind buying frozen as the flavor remains just as good as that of a fresh fish.

SERVES: 4

Preparation time: 15 minutes plus
 20 minutes marinating time
Cooking time: 25 minutes

3 Tbsp teriyaki sauce
2 Tbsp red curry paste
2 Tbsp caster sugar
8 kaffir lime leaves
4 tsp chopped cilantro
4 tsp chopped green onions
2 mangoes, chopped
4 thick pieces of cod (10oz each)
4 large banana leaves
4 blanched savoy cabbage leaves

Salsa
1 red onion, finely chopped
2 Tbsp finely chopped cilantro
1 mango, finely chopped
2 Tbsp extra virgin olive oil
1 avocado, finely chopped
juice of 1 lemon
juice of 1 lime
salt and freshly ground black pepper

method

1 First make the marinade: combine the teriyaki sauce, curry paste, sugar, lime leaves, half the cilantro and half the green onions, and the chopped mango. Add the cod to the marinade and leave for 15–20 minutes. Preheat the oven to 375°F.

2 To make the salsa, mix together all the ingredients in a bowl and leave in the refrigerator until ready to use.

3 Remove the fish steaks from the marinade, place each onto the center of a banana leaf, and cover with remaining marinade. Wrap the edges of the leaves over the fish and secure in place with a toothpick.

4 Bake the fish in the oven for 15 minutes, then open the parcels and return them to the oven for a further 10 minutes.

5 To serve, place each fish steak on a blanched savoy cabbage leaf, sprinkle with the remaining cilantro and green onions and serve immediately with the salsa.

Alternative fish:
black cod, sea bass

1 Place the fish fillet in a deep pan of boiling liquid; make sure there is enough liquid to cover all the fillets. Simmer for about 10 minutes.

Carp poached in beer

This is a very simple recipe but it is delicious. Another good way of cooking this fish is to deep-fry it in beer batter, but this recipe is definitely healthier for you.

SERVES: 4

Preparation time: 5 minutes
Cooking time: 30 minutes

2 x 10fl oz bottles beer
1 medium onion, sliced
1 garlic clove, crushed
2 bay leaves
2 stalks celery, diced
2 tsp salt
1 tsp cracked black pepper
4 carp fillets (6oz each)
1 lemon, quartered
sliced roasted potatoes to serve
    (optional)

method

1 Pour the beer into a deep skillet and add the onion, garlic, bay leaves, celery, and salt and pepper.

2 Bring to a boil and simmer for 10 minutes, then add the carp and lemon and simmer for a further 12 minutes.

3 Remove the carp and reduce the beer by three quarters. Pour over the fish and serve on top of sliced roasted potatoes if desired.

Alternative fish:
trout, catfish, eel

Sour orange pollock

This is a good dish to share in the middle of the table when you have friends around. It is a fairly mild curry so feel free to add extra chilies if you want to give it a little kick!

SERVES: 4

Preparation time: 10 minutes
Cooking time: 25 minutes

1¼ cups fish stock
pinch of sea salt
6 savoy cabbage leaves
    (or Chinese leaves), torn
1 tsp nam pla (fish sauce)
4 pollock fillets (6oz each)
mint leaves
cooked coconut rice to serve

Curry paste
4 large chilies, seeded and chopped
4 shallots, chopped
2 garlic cloves, chopped
1 Tbsp shrimp paste
½ tsp salt
½ tsp sugar
½ tsp turmeric
2 Tbsp ground nut or sesame oil
½ tsp chopped fresh gingerroot

method

1 Blend all the curry paste ingredients until smooth, transfer to a pan, and bring to a boil. Cook for 3 minutes, stirring continuously.

2 Add half the fish stock and a pinch of sea salt, bring back to a boil, then add the cabbage and cook for a further 8 minutes. Add remaining stock and the fish sauce, bring back to a boil, and cook for 5 minutes.

3 Add the pollock fillets and simmer for 4–5 minutes. Remove the cooked fish and keep warm. Add mint leaves to the sauce and cook for 4 minutes.

4 To serve, divide the coconut rice between 4 serving plates, pour over the curry sauce, and top with the fish.

Alternative fish:
cod, codling, monkfish

Left: Carp poached in beer

Steamed sea bass with Thai herbs

You can't really go wrong when cooking sea bass as it is such a great fish. Try and find wild sea bass in the summer season, as the taste is much stronger and the flesh is much firmer.

SERVES: 4

Preparation time: 5 minutes
Cooking time: 20 minutes

1 tsp grated fresh gingerroot
1 tsp chopped cilantro
1 tsp finely chopped lemongrass
1 tsp nam pla (fish sauce)
pinch of brown sugar
1 bunch green onions, finely chopped
1 chili, finely chopped
4 banana leaves
4 sea bass fillets (7oz each)
soy sauce and steamed bok choy to
    serve (optional)

Alternative fish:
sea bream,
gray mullet

method

1 In a bowl stir together the ginger, cilantro, lemongrass, fish sauce, sugar, green onions, and chili until well combined.

2 Line the bottom of a steamer with banana leaves and place the fish fillets on top. Cover the top of the fillets with the herb mixture, making sure they are well coated. Steam the fish for 20 minutes.

3 Serve on top of the banana leaves with a little soy sauce and some steamed bok choy if desired.

Spiced monkfish wrapped in Chinese cabbage

Monkfish is a very ugly looking fish so you never see it in supermarkets with the head still on. It is a great firm fish for roasting, very much like meat. This recipe, which would also be great served with bok choy or stir-fried vegetables, came from London's Chinatown, where I tend to eat quite often.

SERVES: 4

Preparation time: 15 minutes
Cooking time: 20 minutes

½-inch piece fresh gingerroot, peeled and finely chopped
2 whole chilies, finely chopped
2 stalks lemongrass, finely chopped
2 Tbsp chopped cilantro
2 Tbsp sesame oil
1 tsp soy sauce
7oz Chinese cabbage, blanched
2 monkfish fillets (10½oz each)
mashed potatoes or salad to serve (optional)

method

1 Preheat the oven to 350°F. Blend the ginger, chili, lemongrass, cilantro, sesame oil, and soy sauce in a food processor.

2 Take a large sheet of plastic wrap and place the Chinese cabbage leaves on top in an overlapping fashion. Place the monkfish in the middle of the leaves and brush with the herb mixture. Pour over any remaining herb mixture. Wrap the leaves around the fish and then wrap the plastic wrap over the whole parcel. Place this on a large piece of aluminum foil, wrap around the monkfish, and pinch at both ends to form a sausage shape.

3 Bake the parcel in the oven for 20 minutes, then remove from the oven and remove and discard foil and plastic wrap. Slice the monkfish into medallions and pour the cooking juices over the fish. Serve with mashed potatoes or salad if desired.

Alternative fish:
sea bass, swordfish, tuna

Sea robin bouillabaisse

Where I grew up in Italy this fish was very popular, but elsewhere it is less so, mainly because of all the bones. It is, however, great for soups and stews. In season, it is fantastic just roasted with some garlic and potatoes.

SERVES: 4

Preparation time: 10 minutes
Cooking time: 40 minutes

½ cup olive oil
3 onions, finely chopped
2 garlic cloves, chopped
2 leeks, chopped (white part only)
1lb fresh ripe tomatoes, peeled
   and chopped
2 quarts fish stock
2 large pinches of saffron
2 bay leaves
2 sprigs fresh thyme

Alternative fish:
gray mullet, sea bream

3½lb sea robin meat, chopped into
   chunks
4 potatoes, peeled and sliced fairly
   thickly
salt and freshly ground black pepper
pinch of cayenne pepper

method

1 In a large pan, heat the oil and then add the onions, garlic, leeks, and tomatoes and cook until soft. Add the fish stock, saffron, bay leaves, and thyme and boil for 15–20 minutes. Lower the heat and then add the fish and potatoes.

2 Simmer for 5–8 minutes, removing the fish as it is cooked and keeping it on the side; cook until the potatoes are very tender and falling apart. Season with salt, pepper, and cayenne.

3 Divide the fish stew between 4 bowls. If you prefer, you could strain the the stew into bowls and serve as a soup with garlic croutons.

Fish pie

This is a great alternative to shepherd's pie but a lot lighter. Fish pie is a great comfort food and I highly recommend this recipe for those chilly winter nights.

SERVES: 4

Preparation time: 20 minutes
Cooking time: 35 minutes

9oz cod fillets
8oz smoked haddock or cod fillets
⅔ cup milk
⅔ cup water
1 tsp black peppercorns
1 lemon, cut in half
1 bay leaf
1 sprig lemon thyme
6 Tbsp unsalted butter
2 Tbsp flour
3 Tbsp freshly chopped parsley
salt and freshly ground black pepper
1lb potatoes, peeled and cut into
    quarters
about 3 Tbsp milk
4oz raw salmon, diced
4oz raw shrimp, chopped
3 eggs, hard boiled and roughly
    chopped
4oz grated cheese

Alternative fish:
any fish fillets,
including smoked
(e.g. herring,
mackerel, sardine)

method

1 Place the cod, smoked fish, milk, water, peppercorns, lemon, bay leaf, and thyme in a saucepan and bring to a boil. Reduce the heat and simmer for 8 minutes until the fish is nearly cooked. Strain, reserving the cooking liquid. When the fish is cool, remove skin and bones and flake the flesh into a bowl. Preheat the oven to 400°F.

2 Melt 2 tablespoons of the butter in a small pan and add the flour. Stir continuously and cook for about 1 minute. Gradually add the reserved cooking liquid, stirring (or whisking) all the time to prevent it becoming lumpy. Stir in the parsley and season with salt and pepper.

3 Meanwhile cook the potatoes in boiling water until soft (about 10–15 minutes), then drain and mash with 2 tablespoons of butter and about 3 tablespoons of milk and season to taste.

4 Add the raw salmon and shrimp to the cooked fish and then add the eggs and white sauce. Mix together using a wooden spoon and transfer to an ovenproof dish.

5 Spread the mashed potato over the fish mixture, dot with the remaining butter, and sprinkle with grated cheese. Cook for about 20–25 minutes until the top is golden and the inside bubbling.

1 Dip the fish fillet in flour, breadcrumbs or ground nuts. Make sure it is completely coated on both sides.

2 Heat some oil or butter in a deep, non-stick skillet until very hot. Carefully lay the fillet in the oil and sauté for about 7 minutes.

3 Using a slotted spoon turn the fish fillet carefully and cook the other side for about 7 minutes.

4 Once golden brown, lift off the pan using a slotted spoon or spatula and allow oil to drain off.

Catfish in cornmeal

This is not a fish I would normally choose to serve in my restaurants, but after we shot the photo opposite, I put this dish on the menu and it worked a treat with the customers. Catfish is very widely eaten across the USA; let's hope it catches on in the rest of the world too. Ask your fish store to prepare the fish for you as there is a lot to do to it.

SERVES: 4

Preparation time: 10 minutes
Cooking time: 15 minutes

¼ cup cornmeal
2 Tbsp finely ground pine nuts
2 Tbsp flour
pinch of salt
½ tsp cayenne pepper
½ tsp cumin
4 catfish fillets (6oz each)
¼ cup olive oil
minted new potatoes and balsamic
    vinegar to serve (optional)

method

1 In a flat dish combine the cornmeal, pine nuts, flour, salt, cayenne pepper, and cumin.

2 Dip the catfish fillets in the cornmeal mixture, making sure they are well coated, and place them on another plate.

3 Heat the oil in a heavy-based skillet until very hot. Lay the catfish fillets in the oil and sauté for about 7 minutes on each side or until golden brown. Serve with minted new potatoes and balsamic vinegar, if desired..

Alternative fish:
tuna, shark, swordfish, barracuda

SKINNING SALT COD

1 Lay the rehydrated cod on the board skin side down and with a knife lift up the fat and cut it away from the flesh of the fish.

2 Remove all the fat down the side so that you end up with a trimmed fillet. Discard the fat.

3 Insert a sharp knife between the skin and the fish and cut along the skin, lifting the fillet off as you go along.

4 Cut the fish into bite-size pieces ready to make your stew, or cut it into large fillet portions to pan-fry, roast, or grill.

Salt cod caldeirada

I picked this recipe up on holiday in Portugal and was inspired to make my own version of it. I hope you enjoy making it for friends—it's superb for Sunday lunch.

SERVES: 4

Preparation time: 10 minutes
Cooking time: 1 hour

1 Tbsp extra virgin olive oil
2 garlic cloves, finely chopped
1 large white onion, sliced
6 potatoes
8 tomatoes
1 spicy chorizo sausage
8 raw jumbo shrimp
1½lb salt cod, rehydrated
½ tsp paprika
2 bay leaves
1 tsp oregano
chopped parsley to serve

method

1 In a large deep saucepan, heat the olive oil and pan-fry the garlic and onion for 1 minute over a medium heat. Remove from the heat.

2 Peel and slice the potatoes into ¾-inch widths, peel and roughly chop the tomatoes, slice the chorizo sausage, and peel and devein the jumbo shrimp. Cut the rehydrated salt cod into large chunks.

3 Add the potatoes, tomatoes, chorizo sausage, shrimp, and salt cod to the pan, along with the paprika, bay leaves, and oregano. Pour in enough water to just cover the ingredients.

4 Return to the heat and simmer for 1 hour until the potatoes are tender. Serve scattered with chopped parsley.

Alternative fish:
monkfish, John Dory, bream

1 Place the salt cod in a bowl of cold water and leave to soak for 24 hours to rehydrate it and remove salt. Change the water frequently.

2 Cook fish in a saucepan of fresh boiling water for 20–30 minutes. Drain and cool, remove skin and bones, and flake the fish into a bowl.

3 Add the remaining ingredients to the bowl and mash until all the ingredients are combined.

4 Flour your hands and, taking a handful of fish mixture at a time, roll it into a ball. Gently flatten it to make a round "cake".

Salt cod fish cakes with parsley sauce

This is one of my favorite photos in the book: I love the crunchy vegetables the fish cakes are served with. This is a great dish to serve a family and you can vary it by serving the fish cakes with chili sauce instead of this parsley one.

SERVES: 4

Preparation time: 15 minutes plus 24 hours soaking time
Cooking time: 1 hour

9oz salt cod
1lb potatoes, peeled and chopped
½ tsp cayenne pepper
1 chili, seeded and finely chopped
3 garlic cloves, finely chopped
2 Tbsp finely chopped parsley
¼ cup light cream
2 egg yolks
⅔ cup plain flour
1 Tbsp olive oil
½ cup butter
stir-fried vegetables to serve

Parsley sauce

3 Tbsp unsalted butter
¼ cup plain flour
1¼ cups milk, warm
1¼ cups fish stock, warm
⅓ cup finely chopped parsley
salt and freshly ground black pepper

method

1 Soak the cod in cold water for at least 24 hours, changing the water 4 or 5 times.

2 Drain the fish and place in a saucepan, cover with fresh water, and simmer over medium heat for 20–30 minutes until it is cooked. Drain and, when cool, flake the fish into a large bowl, making sure to remove the skin and any bones.

3 Meanwhile cook the potatoes in salted water for 10–15 minutes until they are soft. Drain and push potatoes through a strainer or a potato ricer.

4 Add the potato to the cod along with the cayenne pepper, chili, garlic, parsley, cream, and egg yolks and mix well to combine. Flour your hands and then pick up some of the fish mixture and roll it in your hands to make a ball. On a floured board, flatten the ball down slightly to make a fish cake shape—you can make either two small fish cakes or one large one per person. These can be covered and kept in the refrigerator for up to 12 hours before cooking.

5 To make the parsley sauce, melt the butter in a saucepan over a low heat and then stir in the flour using a wooden spoon to make a roux. Gradually add the warm milk and fish stock a little at a time, stirring continuously to make sure the sauce is smooth with no lumps. Bring to a boil and, continuing to stir, simmer the sauce for 5 minutes until smooth and creamy. Remove from the heat, add the parsley, and season to taste. (This can be reheated when you need it.)

6 Pan-fry the fish cakes in the olive oil and butter over a medium heat for about 15 minutes (depending on the size of your fish cakes), turning once, until golden brown. Serve on top of some stir-fried seasonal vegetables with the sauce poured around.

Alternative fish:
cod, salmon, crab meat

Sashimi of sea bass

Sashimi is any kind of fresh, raw fillet of fish that is not served with rice—other sushi are served either with or on rice. Make sure that you ask your fish store for sushi-grade fish when you are making this recipe; this will guarantee the freshness of the fish. It is important to find very fresh fish for sashimi dishes.

SERVES: 4

Preparation time: 10 minutes plus
   45 minutes marinating time

6oz very fresh sea bass
3 Tbsp soy sauce
1 tsp wasabi
2 ripe avocados
4 shiso leaves, crumbled
1 Tbsp toasted sesame seeds

method

1 Slice the sea bass very thinly.

2 Mix together the soy and wasabi and marinate the sea bass in this mixture.

3 Pit and peel the avocado and cut into chunks.

4 Lay the sea bass on a flat plate and place the avocado on top. Sprinkle with the shiso and sesame seeds. Pour over some of the marinade before eating.

Alternative fish:
salmon, tuna

Smoked haddock and avocado mousse

Smoked fish is quite under-rated nowadays: I remember it as a delicacy and still treat it like one. When I was working in the south of France this recipe was always on the menu; I decided to include it here as it's a great, easy recipe.

SERVES: 4

Preparation time: 20 minutes
Cooking time: 15 minutes
Chilling time: 1 hour

8oz smoked haddock fillets, skinned
½ white onion, cut into rings
2 Tbsp unsalted butter
salt and freshly ground black pepper
1 bay leaf
⅔ cup fish stock
1 ripe avocado, pitted, peeled, and
   chopped
1 Tbsp granulated gelatin
2 Tbsp white wine
7 Tbsp heavy cream
1 egg white
cucumber, tomato and red onion
   salad to serve (optional)

method

1 Place the fish in a shallow pan and top with the onion rings. Dot with the butter, season with pepper, and add the bay leaf and stock. Poach for about 4 minutes until the fish flakes with a fork. Remove the fish, reserving the cooking liquid, and set aside to cool.

2 Remove the onion and bay leaf from the cooking liquid and boil until it has reduced by two thirds. Flake the fish into a food processor, add the cooking liquid, and blend until smooth. Transfer the fish to a large bowl and stir in the chopped avocado.

3 In a small saucepan, sprinkle the gelatin over 2 tablespoons of cold water and leave until it becomes spongy. Add the wine and heat until it is completely dissolved, stirring continuously. Pour into the fish and mix in well.

4 Whip the cream in a bowl. In another bowl, beat the egg white with a little salt until stiff, then fold in the cream. Fold this mixture into the fish and season to taste. Pour either into individual ramekins or into a large dish, cover with plastic wrap, and leave in the refrigerator for at least 1 hour. Serve with cucumber, tomato, and red onion salad if desired.

Alternative fish:
smoked mackerel

Chinese squid

This dish is one of my best sellers in Zilli Fish and very popular at the annual event La Dolce Vita and at Taste of London: people now phone to book their portion just to make sure we have enough for them!

SERVES: 4

Preparation time: 10 minutes
Cooking time: 4–5 minutes

1 Tbsp olive oil
3 tsp sesame oil
4 squid, cleaned and cut into rings
  (see page 44)
½ tsp finely chopped fresh
  gingerroot
2 Tbsp chopped cilantro
1 red chili, seeded and finely
  chopped
3 green onions, finely chopped
1 stalk lemongrass, finely chopped
2 Tbsp soy sauce

method

1 Heat the olive oil and sesame oil in a wok or large skillet, add the squid, and stir-fry for about 2–3 minutes.

2 Mix together the ginger, cilantro, chili, green onions, lemongrass, and 1 teaspoon of soy sauce and add to the squid. Stir-fry for 1 minute until the herbs and squid are well mixed and hot. Stir in the rest of the soy sauce just before serving.

Alternative fish:
jumbo shrimp, cuttlefish

1 Rinse the squid thoroughly in cold water. The squid should not smell of fish at all; if it does, it is not fresh and should not be eaten.

2 Holding the body of the squid firmly in one hand, grasp the base of the tentacles and pull away from the body to remove the entrails.

3 Still holding onto the body, place your hand in the cavity of the squid and remove the "plastic" backbone or quill.

4 Take a sharp knife and cut through the eyes on the tentacles.

5 Using both hands, turn the squid tentacles almost inside out.

6 Using your thumb, push through the bottom of the tentacles until the "third" eye pops out. Discard this.

7 Firmly grasping the wings, push your fingers between the wings and body of the squid and pull. This will remove the wings and most of the skin.

8 Pull the remaining skin off the squid, making sure you end up with a clean, white body.

9 With a thumb or finger, make an indentation in the bottom of the squid. Remove your thumb and place a small carrot in this indentation.

10 Using the carrot, turn the squid inside out, remove the carrot, and clean off any insides and membrane from the squid.

11 Using scissors or a sharp knife, cut off both ends of the squid, then cut along the natural indentation in the squid.

12 Place the squid with the whiter inside up on a board. Using a knife score it diagonally until you have a cross hatch pattern.

Grilled squid with sweet chili sauce and arugula

This is my favorite way of cooking squid: the flavor of the squid can be lost in the oil when you fry it. Make sure that you don't overcook the squid or it will become tough. Scoring the inside of the squid helps it to cook evenly.

SERVES: 4

Preparation time: 10 minutes
Cooking time: 6 minutes

4 squid (12oz each), cleaned
⅓ cup extra virgin olive oil
sea salt flakes and freshly ground
   black pepper
2 Tbsp balsamic vinegar
9oz wild arugula, washed and
   drained
lemon wedges to serve

Alternative fish:
octopus (cook for at least
5 minutes)

Chili sauce
2 Tbsp nam pla (fish sauce)
2 Tbsp water
4 red chilies, finely chopped
juice of 1 lemon
1 tsp brown sugar

method

1 Using a thin knife, score the inside of the squid to form a cross hatch pattern (see step 12 opposite).

2 Heat a grill pan to medium-hot. Place the squid, scored side down, on the pan, and brush with a little of the oil, then sprinkle with salt and pepper. Grill for 4–5 minutes, turn over, brush with more oil and season. Grill for a further 3–4 minutes until squid begins to curl up at the edges and is tender. Slice each in half.

3 Meanwhile make the chili sauce: in a food processor, combine the fish sauce, water, chili, lemon juice, and sugar and process for about 2–3 minutes until the dressing is smooth.

4 Place the remainder of the olive oil and the balsamic vinegar in a screw-top jar and shake vigorously to combine. Season to taste. Place the arugula in a large bowl and pour over the oil and vinegar dressing. Distribute the arugula between 4 plates and arrange the hot squid on top. Spoon over the chili sauce and serve with lemon wedges.

Dover sole

Plaice

English sole

Halibut

Brill

Flat Fish

Turbot

Flat Fish

Flat fish are strange-looking creatures, most of which are found in the Atlantic. All species start life with an eye on each side of their head like round fish. At this stage they swim upright near the surface. As they mature, one eye moves around so that both eyes are on top of the head. This enables them to move along the sea bed, feeding on whatever passes by, while keeping a look out for predators. Flat fish also have the ability to change their color to blend in with their surroundings. Because they do not have to chase their food—or flee predators—their flesh is always delicate and white without too much muscle and fiber. They have a simple bone structure, so even people nervous of bones can cope with them. The best way of eating most flat fish is pan-fried with a little lemon, parsley, and browned butter—stonger flavors will overpower the delicate flavor of these fish. The exceptions are plaice, which needs a bit more flavoring and is delicious cooked in breadcrumbs, and halibut, which is best cooked in a sauce to keep it moist. Good rich sauces for this fish include hollandaise, parsley, and lobster.

BRILL *Schopthalmus rhombus* or *Rhombus laevis*
Brill is similar to turbot in both appearance and taste but is regarded as the poor relation, a reputation that is unjustified as it has a fine, softish white flesh with a delicate flavor. The top of the fish has dark gray skin with small scales and the underbelly is either creamy or a pinkish white.

DOVER SOLE *Solea solea* and *Solea vulgaris*
Widely regarded as the best fish of all, Dover sole has a firm, delicate flesh with a superb flavor. The Dover sole has a well-proportioned oval shape with a grayish or light brown skin and eyes on the righthand side of its head. Most Dover sole weigh between 7oz and 1lb 5oz.

ENGLISH SOLE *Microstomus kitt*
This fish is actually related to the dab, plaice, and flounder and not, as you might expect, to the Dover sole. The English sole is oval in shape with smooth, reddish brown skin, a very small head, and bulging eyes. Its flesh is soft and white and similar to that of plaice but of a superior quality. English sole, which is also known as English sole, is an extremely good alternative to the more expensive Dover sole.

FLOUNDER *Platichthys flesus*
This famous saltwater fish, also known as fluke, is a dull brown-gray or green on its upper side with a white underbelly. Flounder is similar to plaice and, like plaice, is best eaten as soon as possible after being caught. It is often considered to be the "fish for people who don't like fish" and is sought after by both anglers and restaurateurs. The best way to cook flounder is to either steam it or sauté it.

HALIBUT *Hippoglossus hippoglossus*
The largest of all the flat fish—it can grow up to 6½ft in length and weigh more than 440lb—the halibut is found in very cold, deep waters. It has an elongated, greenish brown body, pointed head, white underbelly, and, as with most flat fish, eyes on the righthand side of its head. The flesh is fine, with a meaty texture and a delicious flavor.

PLAICE *Pleuronectes platessa*
This is a very distinctive looking fish that has a smooth, dark grayish-brown skin with orange spots on the top and a completely white underbelly. As with most flat fish, the eyes are on the righthand side of the head. Plaice has a soft, white flesh that can be fairly bland in flavor. An average plaice weighs between 14oz and 2lb 4oz and can live for up to 50 years.

SKATE *Rajus batis*
This flat seawater fish lives in cold and temperate waters on the bottom of the sea where its coloring—a gray or brown back with lighter spots and black dots—camouflages it on the sea bed. Skates lay eggs in rectangular cases with "tassels" in each corner, which when washed up on the beach are known as "mermaids' purses." When alive, skates contain little ammonia, but after death they produce a lot more. The smell of ammonia should disappear when the skate is cooked; if it doesn't, the skate is not fresh.

TURBOT *Psetta maxima* and *Scophthalmus maximus*
While not the most attractive of fish, the turbot makes up for its strange appearance with its superb texture and taste; indeed, it is a very close contender to the Dover sole. The turbot has a very tough, warty flesh, a small head, and a large body. Unlike other flat fish, its underbelly is sometimes gray. The flesh is creamy white, with a firm, dense texture and a lovely sweet flavor.

Mediterranean-style brill

I love brill: it is not a cheap fish but it has a great texture. This recipe reminds me of my early years of cooking fish and is simplicity at its best.

Alternative fish:
sole, plaice

SERVES: 4

Preparation time: 10 minutes
Cooking time: 25 minutes

4 brill (10oz each), cleaned
4 garlic cloves
1 cup black olives
3 cups cherry tomatoes
2 Tbsp shredded basil
4 fresh anchovies in oil, drained
1 Tbsp capers
⅓ cup extra virgin olive oil
⅓ cup white wine
1 Tbsp chopped fresh
   parsley

method

1 Preheat the oven to 375°F. Rinse the fish under cold running water and with a sharp knife slash the skin of each fish a few times on both sides.

2 Place the fish in a roasting pan with the garlic, olives, cherry tomatoes, 1 tablespoon of basil, anchovies, capers, and olive oil and cook in the oven for 15 minutes.

3 Add the white wine to the roasting pan and cook for a further 10 minutes.

4 Remove from the oven and serve sprinkled with chopped fresh parsley and the remainder of the shredded basil.

Skate with black butter

These skate wings are pan-fried, but you can also roast them. If you do so, watch the edges as they tend to burn. Cover them with foil and the skate will cook quite quickly.

SERVES: 4

Preparation time: 5 minutes plus
   1 hour soaking time
Cooking time: 15 minutes

4 skate wings (8oz each)
¼ cup red wine vinegar
½ cup seasoned flour
olive oil for pan-frying
salt and freshly ground black pepper
2 Tbsp chopped fresh parsley
⅔ cup butter
2 Tbsp drained capers

Alternative fish:
Dover sole, flounder, dab

method

1 Put the skate in a large shallow dish, cover with water, and add a pinch of salt and a tablespoon of the vinegar. Leave to soak for 1 hour to remove any impurities, then rinse.

2 Dip the skate wings in the flour and then pan-fry them in some olive oil, turning them occasionally, for about 15 minutes, depending on the size of the wings.

3 Remove the skate to a warm serving dish, season with salt and pepper, and scatter parsley over.

4 Meanwhile, in a small pan, heat the butter until it foams and turns a rich brown color. Add the capers and warm through, then pour over the skate and serve immediately.

Dover sole with peas and tomato sauce

What puzzles me about this fish is that it is local to the UK yet is always so expensive. Dover sole also tastes great simply grilled or roasted and served with lemon oil dressing.

SERVES: 4

Preparation time: 5 minutes
Cooking time: 35 minutes

6 Tbsp olive oil
1 red onion, finely chopped
3 garlic cloves, crushed
3 Tbsp Italian flat-leaf parsley
pinch of fennel seeds
1 glass dry white wine
14oz can chopped tomatoes
salt and freshly ground black pepper
2 cups shelled peas
4 whole Dover sole (14oz each)
¼ cup butter

method

1 Heat 4 tablespoons of oil in a pan and add the onion, garlic, parsley, and fennel seeds. Cook until the onions are translucent. Remove the garlic at this stage.

2 Add the wine to the pan and cook until it has evaporated, then add the chopped tomatoes and cook over a medium heat for 8 minutes until the sauce begins to thicken. Add salt and pepper and peas and cook over a low heat for 12 minutes.

3 Pan-fry the Dover sole in 2 tablespoons of olive oil for 10 minutes on each side. Just before they are cooked, add the butter to the pan. Serve the fish with the tomato and pea sauce.

Alternative fish:
plaice, English sole

Right: Skate with black butter

1 You can obtain 4 fillets from a flat fish but they will not be identical in size because of the irregular shape of the fish.

2 Using a sharp knife or pair of scissors, remove the fins from either side of the fish's body.

3 Cut across the base of the tail with a sharp knife until you reach the bone.

4 Grip the fish firmly by the tail with one hand and with your other hand pull the skin away from you and off the fish.

Dover sole fillets Dijon

When I was working in the South of France this dish was regularly featured on the menu and was always extremely popular, so I am now sharing it with you.

SERVES: 4

Preparation time: 10 minutes
Cooking time: 30 minutes

2 Tbsp butter
2 Tbsp extra virgin olive oil
4 Dover sole fillets (7oz each) or
    4 whole Dover sole (14oz each)

Shrimp sauce
2 Tbsp unsalted butter
1 Tbsp olive oil
1 garlic clove, crushed
6oz raw medium shrimp
¼ cup white wine
¾ cup heavy cream
1 Tbsp chopped dill
1 Tbsp Dijon mustard
1 Tbsp lemon juice
salt and freshly ground black pepper
spinach with celery and red bell
    peppers to serve (optional)

method

1 Heat the butter and oil in a pan, then add the fish and cook over a medium heat for about 6 minutes on each side until golden brown and cooked through. Transfer to a warm oven until the sauce is ready.

2 To make the sauce: melt the butter and oil in a pan and add the crushed garlic. Cook gently for 1 minute until the garlic is golden then remove it from the pan. (Be careful not to burn the garlic as this will ruin the sauce.)

3 Add the shrimp to the pan and cook for 3 minutes or until they change to a nice pink color. Add the wine and cook until almost completely evaporated, then stir in the cream, dill, mustard, and lemon juice, warm through, and season to taste. Serve sauce with the fish, with spinach, celery, and red bell peppers if desired.

Alternative fish:
English sole, halibut, plaice

5 Pull the roe out of the fish; it should come away in one long piece.

6 Using a sharp knife and starting from the head, cut down the back bone of the fish. Then lay the knife as close to the bone as you can.

7 Cut down toward the tail using long stroking movements to remove the first fillet. Repeat this process for the other 3 fillets.

English sole rolls stuffed with leeks, carrots, and shrimp

English sole fillets are one of the specialties of my restaurant and well liked by my customers. If you love sole, this is the recipe for you—simple and fantastic.

SERVES: 4

Preparation time: 10 minutes
Cooking time: 25 minutes

3 carrots, grated
1 leek, grated or finely chopped
5 Tbsp breadcrumbs
6oz finely chopped shrimp
1 Tbsp lemon juice
salt and freshly ground black pepper
6 English sole fillets (9oz each)
1 Tbsp olive oil
lemon oil
grilled Portobello mushrooms and
    sautéed red cabbage to serve
    (optional)

Alternative fish:
plaice, brill, Dover sole

method

1 Preheat the oven to 400°F.

2 In a bowl mix together the carrots, leek, breadcrumbs, and shrimp. Add the lemon juice and season with salt and pepper.

3 Lay the fish fillets skin side up (make sure this is the white skin and not the spotted/dark skin) on a board. Place one quarter of the filling near the end of one fillet and, using your fingers to ensure the filling stays in place, carefully roll up the fillet to make a round parcel. Repeat with remaining English sole fillets and filling.

4 Place the rolls on a baking sheet and sprinkle with olive oil. Cover with aluminum foil and cook in the oven for 25 minutes.

5 Serve the English sole rolls drizzled with lemon oil and on a bed of grilled Portobello mushrooms and sautéed red cabbage if desired.

1 Lay a piece of parchment paper on a board and place fish and other ingredients in the center. Fold up all edges to make a parcel.

English sole in parchment

I love the fact that this recipe contains lots of vegetables! Try to include a variety of seasonal vegetables in the parcel—any combination will work.

SERVES: 4

Preparation time: 15 minutes
Cooking time: 10 minutes

2 carrots, cut into thin strips
2 zucchini, cut into thin strips
2 leeks, cut into thin strips
1 fennel bulb, cut into thin strips
1 green bell pepper, cut into thin
    strips
2 tomatoes, peeled, seeded, and
    diced
salt and freshly ground black pepper
2 Tbsp chopped fresh tarragon
4 English sole fillets (7oz each), cut
    in half, or 8 fillets if quite small
3 Tbsp olive oil
¼ cup Champagne or sparkling wine

method

1 Preheat the oven to 375°F. Cut 4 pieces of non-stick baking parchment or rice paper about 18 inches square, fold each piece in half and, using the fold as the center line, cut out a half heart shape.

2 Open the paper hearts and distribute the carrot, zucchini, leek, fennel, and bell pepper strips and the diced tomatoes between them, placing them in the fold of each heart. Sprinkle the vegetables with salt and pepper and half the tarragon. Arrange 2 pieces of fish over each bed. Sprinkle with the remaining tarragon, the olive oil, and wine.

3 Fold the top half of the paper heart over the fish and vegetables, fold the edges over, and twist and roll the paper to form an airtight parcel.

4 Put the parcels onto a baking sheet and bake in the oven for 10 minutes, or until the paper is brown and well puffed out. Serve the fish and vegetables still in their parchment parcels.

Alternative fish:
haddock, scallops, halibut

Halibut with saffron sauce and stewed leeks

If available, halibut is a great fish for this recipe and the leeks work much better with it than onions. The soft, lighter flavor of the leeks really complements this fish: anything too heavy would kill the fish's delicate flavor.

SERVES: 4

Preparation time: 10 minutes
Cooking time: 25 minutes

4 halibut fillets (6oz each)
2 pinches of saffron
1¾ cups fish stock
1 cup white wine
7oz leeks, cut into 4-inch lengths
¼ cup butter
salt and freshly ground black pepper
1 tsp lemon juice
chopped green onions to serve

method

1 Preheat the oven to 375°F.

2 Place the fish in an ovenproof dish, season, add saffron, and pour over fish stock and wine. Poach in the oven for 8 minutes.

3 Drain the liquid from the dish into a saucepan and add the leeks. Keep the fish warm. Cook the leeks gently until soft, about 15 minutes. Add the butter, seasoning, and lemon juice and stir until butter has melted.

4 Remove leeks with a slotted spoon and divide between 4 plates, place fish on top and pour saffron sauce over. Sprinkle with chopped green onions and serve.

Alternative fish:
turbot, monkfish, cod, salmon

Flounder with grapes, golden raisins, and balsamic vinegar

The inspiration for this recipe came when I was on vacation in South Africa, where they tend to marry fish with fruit a lot. The sweetness of the fruit is offset by the sharpness of the balsamic vinegar. This is a really light, well-balanced dish, which tastes particularly fine when served with an arugula salad.

SERVES: 4

Preparation time: 10 minutes
Cooking time: 15 minutes

4 flounder fillets (6oz each)
salt and freshly ground black pepper
juice of 1 lemon
2 Tbsp butter
½ cup golden raisins
¾ cup seedless grapes
2 Tbsp freshly chopped parsley
3 Tbsp balsamic vinegar
⅓ cup marsala wine

method

1 Preheat the oven to 400°F. Arrange the fish in a shallow baking dish, sprinkle with salt, pepper, and lemon juice and dot with the butter.

2 In a bowl, stir together the golden raisins, grapes, parsley, balsamic vinegar, and marsala wine. Spoon a quarter of this mixture over each fillet and bake in the oven for 15 minutes.

Alternative fish:
salmon, sea bass, turbot

Right: Flounder with grapes, golden raisins, and balsamic vinegar

Halibut with lemon, red onion, and cilantro

I have tested this recipe over and over again with my customers and it's always a winner.
Don't forget to add plenty of cilantro—what a great herb!

SERVES: 4

Preparation time: 10 minutes plus
   1 hour marinating time
Cooking time: 15 minutes

juice of 1 lemon
1 tsp chopped garlic
1 tsp paprika
1 tsp ground cumin
1 tsp chopped fresh tarragon
salt and freshly ground black pepper
4 halibut steaks (6oz each)
¼ cup extra virgin olive oil
⅔ cup flour
1¼ cups fish or vegetable stock
1 chili, seeded and chopped
3 Tbsp chopped cilantro
1 red onion, sliced

method

1 Mix the lemon juice, garlic, paprika, cumin, tarragon, and some salt and pepper together in a bowl. Place the halibut in a dish and spoon over this lemon mix. Set aside to marinate for 1 hour.

2 Heat 3 tablespoons of olive oil in a skillet. Dust the fish with flour, add to the pan, and cook over a gentle heat for 3 minutes on one side, then turn the fish over and pan-fry on the other side for a further 2 minutes. Pour over the stock, cover, and simmer for 5 minutes. Add the chili and half the cilantro to the pan and cook for a further 5 minutes. Transfer to a serving dish.

3 Meanwhile heat the remaining olive oil in a separate skillet and sauté the onion until soft. Scatter the sautéed onion over the fish with the remaining cilantro.

Alternative fish:
turbot, sea bass, cod

Turbot hollandaise

This is a very special fish so it deserves a special sauce. A lot of people are nervous about making hollandaise, but it is really very easy and well worth making the effort. This is a great dinner party recipe—simple yet elegant.

SERVES: 4

Preparation time: 10 minutes
Cooking time: 10 minutes

2 Tbsp extra virgin olive oil
4 turbot fillets (6oz each)
1 Tbsp chopped fresh parsley
steamed asparagus spears to serve
   (optional)

Hollandaise sauce
½ cup unsalted butter
1–2 Tbsp lemon juice
2 egg yolks
salt and ground white pepper

method

1 First make the hollandaise sauce: melt the butter in a pan. In a heatproof bowl, mix together the lemon juice and egg yolks. Add salt and pepper and whisk until completely smooth.

2 Place the bowl over a pan of simmering water and slowly pour the melted butter onto the egg-yolk mixture in a steady stream, beating continuously with a wooden spoon to make a smooth, creamy sauce. Add more lemon juice to taste if necessary.

3 Heat the olive oil in a skillet until hot, then add the turbot fillets and pan-fry for 2–3 minutes on each side until cooked through and golden.

4 Serve the fish with the hollandaise poured over and sprinkled with parsley. If necessary you can rehydrate the hollandaise with some warm water. For presentation you could place the dish under a hot broiler so that the hollandaise browns a touch. Serve with asparagus spears, if desired.

Alternative fish:
swordfish, salmon, sea bass

BREADING SOLE OR OTHER FISH FILLETS

1 Place beaten egg in one shallow dish, flour in another, and breadcrumbs in a third. Have your fish fillets ready to dip.

2 Dip each fish fillet in the flour first; this will ensure that the rest of the ingredients stick to the fish.

3 Then dip the fillet into the beaten egg. Make sure it is well covered in egg or the breadcrumbs will not adhere to the fish.

4 Finally place the fillet in the breadcrumbs. Pat the fish down gently with your fingers to ensure it is evenly coated. Turn it over and repeat.

Fried English sole with tomato sauce

I love eating fish in breadcrumbs and English sole is perfect for this recipe: the crispness of the breadcrumbs with the flavorsome tomato sauce is a great combination.

SERVES: 4

Preparation time: 15 minutes
Cooking time: 1 hour 10 minutes

2 Tbsp all-purpose flour
2 eggs, beaten
1 cup breadcrumbs
4 English sole fillets (7oz each)
1 Tbsp butter
1 Tbsp olive oil
1 lemon, cut into wedges, to serve
minted new potatoes to serve

Tomato sauce
2 Tbsp extra virgin olive oil
2 shallots, finely diced
1 garlic clove, finely diced
14oz can chopped tomatoes
8 black olives, cut in half
salt and freshly ground black pepper
1 branch fresh basil leaves

method

1 To make the tomato sauce, heat the olive oil in a large pan, add the shallots and garlic, and cook for about 6 minutes over a low heat. Stir in the tomatoes and simmer, uncovered, for 40 minutes, stirring occasionally. Add olives and cook for a further 5 minutes. Season to taste, tear the basil leaves, and add to the sauce.

2 Spread the flour on a plate and pour the egg mixture into a dish; place the breadcrumbs on another plate. Dip the sole in the flour, then the egg, and then the breadcrumbs, making sure it is well coated.

3 Heat the butter and olive oil in a skillet and pan-fry the sole for 4 minutes on each side until a lovely golden brown.

4 Drain the fish and serve with lemon wedges, tomato sauce, and minted new potatoes.

Alternative fish:
plaice, brill, John Dory

Plaice goujons in sparkling wine batter

Plaice is perfect for this recipe as it has a good firm texture so holds together well. Plaice is not normally regarded as being very special, but I happen to disagree: it is extremely versatile and ranks up there with Dover sole for me.

SERVES: 4

Preparation time: 25 minutes plus
   1 hour resting time for batter
Cooking time: 5 minutes

⅔ cup self-raising flour
½ cup cornstarch
1 tsp salt
1 egg white
1 cup Champagne
seasoned flour for coating
1½lb plaice fillets, cut into goujons
vegetable oil for deep-frying
tartar sauce to serve (optional)

Alternative fish:

codling, cod, English sole

method

1 In a bowl, combine the flour, cornstarch, salt, and egg white. Whisk in the Champagne until you have a smooth batter. Leave in the refrigerator to rest for at least 1 hour.

2 Place some seasoned flour in a shallow dish and dip the goujons into the flour to coat evenly, then dip them into the batter.

3 Heat the vegetable oil in a large pan. Drop the coated goujons directly into the hot oil and cook until crispy and golden brown. Remove goujons from the oil with a slotted spoon and drain on paper towels. Serve immediately, with tartar sauce if desired.

Brown trout

Rainbow trout

Sea trout

Eel

Mackerel

Herring

Sardine

Anchovies

Whitebait

Salmon

Oily Fish

Oily Fish

Oily fish are generally very popular as they are cheap, healthy, and readily available. Oily fish are good for the brain and great at helping to prevent heart attacks and strokes; they can also help make your skin look younger. They are a great source of protein, rich in magnesium, zinc, selenium, and vitamin A, plus B vitamins, and—most importantly—they are a good source of omega 3 fatty acids, which make the blood less "sticky," thus helping to reduce the risk of blood clots that could cause heart attacks. It is a well known fact that people who eat a lot of oily fish, like the Japanese, tend to live longer and have the lowest rates of heart disease. Most oily fish, such as sardines, mackerel, herrings, are quite "fishy" fish, but don't be put off: I think they are the way forward in healthy eating. But aside from all their many healthy benefits, the best thing about oily fish is that they happen to be very good eating. They tend to have no scales so are easy to prepare and for me there is nothing better than a fresh mackerel simply cooked on the grill with lemon and butter—a wonderful lunch or dinner.

ANCHOVY *Engraulis encrasilcolus*
This small fish prefers the warm waters of the Mediterranean. There are various species to be found all round the world, but it is normally about 8 inches long with a green/blue back and a silvery belly. Anchovies are mostly sold canned or bottled in oil; fresh ones are rare.

EEL genus *Anguilla*
Eels could be considered to be marine fish rather than freshwater ones. They start and end their life in the sea, but spend most of their life in fresh water, and this is where they tend to be caught. Eels will live out of water for a long time and then keep well even after death. If you buy live eels, they need to be killed, bled, skinned, cleaned, and cut. This is a very long and complicated process so I recommend that you ask your fish store to do it for you. Eels are relatively fatty fish and make a rich dish.

HERRING *Clupea harengus*
This fish has a dark blue-black back, shading down to silvery white on its belly. An adult herring is about 8–10 inches long. The flesh is fairly fat and for this reason, herrings lend themselves to being pickled.

MACKEREL *Scomber scombrus*
Mackerel are very easy to identify because of their beautiful greeny-blue skin with wavy bands of black, and green backs with silvery bellies. I love mackerel when they are fresh and in their prime, which is normally in late spring and early summer. Mackerel, like most oily fish, is very high in omega 3 oils.

SALMON *Salmo salar*
One of the most widely available and popular fish to be found in markets and supermarkets. Almost all salmon sold is farmed and tends to have firm, pink flesh with not too much fat. Wild salmon, which is available at a higher price, has firmer, deeper pink flesh.

SARDINES *Sardina pilchardus* and *Clupea pilchardus*
Most people assume that sardines and pilchards are different fish. In fact they are not: a pilchard is just a larger sardine. Sardines owe their name to Sardinia, where they were once found in large quantities. Sardines need to be very fresh to be at their best: stay away from any damaged, dull-looking sardines as they will not be great eating. If you want to stuff them, then make sure you choose larger sardines, which will hold together better when you are filling them.

SWORDFISH *Xiphias gladius*
Aptly named after its swordlike nose, which acounts for a third of the size of the fish, the swordfish can be found in all the great oceans. Swordfish have a firm white flesh, which is perfect for steaks.

TROUT
This is the most well known of the freshwater fish and is very popular with fishermen. There are two main types of freshwater trout: rainbow (*Salmo gairdneri*) and brown trout (*Salmo trutta*), both of which can be caught in the wild. However, most commercially available trout have been farmed. Hatchery rainbow trout are fed a caryatid pigment to give them pink flesh; wild rainbow trout have a moist white flesh. Sea trout (also *Salmo trutta*) is similar to salmon in that it is migratory and eats crustaceans that contain the caryatid pigment, which gives the fish its distinctive pink color. Be careful when ordering trout in the southern states of the USA as what is known elsewhere as croaker is called sea trout or trout there.

TUNA genus *Thunnus*
These torpedo-shaped fish have powerful muscles and a firm, dark, meaty flesh. They gather in shoals and migrate toward the shore when breeding where they are then caught in huge numbers by enormous drift-nets. Unfortunately, these nets can also catch dolphin, turtles, and other marine life; "dolphin-friendly" canned tuna has not been caught by drift-net. As with many other popular fish, over fishing is leading to a decline in tuna stocks around the world. The finest of all tuna, bluefin, is normally used for sushi and sashimi and is highly prized in Japan. Bluefin tuna, which is also the largest of the tuna family, has a deep red flesh. Any tuna that has changed to a light brown color should be discarded as this means it is past its prime.

WHITEBAIT
Whitebait is not a species of fish but rather the term used to group any tiny fish—typically "bait" are only 1–2 inches in length. They may be young sprats or herrings or other small fish. Because of their small size, there is no cleaning involved—you eat the entire fish, including head, fins, and gut—but whitebait is very tender and edible.

Mackerel with mustard and lemon butter

This is one of the best ways of cooking mackerel—simple and full of flavor. You can use fillets instead of whole mackerel if you wish: you won't need to score the flesh and they'll need cooking for about 3 minutes on each side.

SERVES: 4

Preparation time: 10 minutes
Cooking time: 20 minutes

4 fresh mackerel (6oz each),
   cleaned
salt and freshly ground black pepper
4 slices lemon
4 sprigs rosemary
½ cup butter, melted
grated zest of 1 lemon
2 Tbsp lemon juice
2 Tbsp wholegrain mustard
3 Tbsp chopped fresh parsley
6 cups baby spinach

method

1 Preheat the broiler. Make 3 slashes into the skin of the fish on either side, then season with salt and pepper. Insert a slice of lemon and a sprig of rosemary into the cavity of each fish.

2 In a bowl, mix together the melted butter, lemon zest and juice, mustard, and parsley; season.

3 Place the mackerel on a broiler rack and brush with the mustard butter. Broil for about 10 minutes on each side, occasionally brushing with more butter.

4 Arrange the baby spinach on 4 plates and place a mackerel on top of each. Heat the remaining mustard butter until bubbling and pour over the fish before serving.

Alternative fish:
sardines, herring

1 Using scissors or a knife, make an incision in the belly toward the tail and cut upward. Pull out the innards and wash the fish in cold water.

2 Using scissors, cut off all the fins. Smooth fish such as mackerel and trout do not need scaling.

3 Insert the edge of a sharp knife by the gills and press down to make an incision.

4 Keeping the knife close to the backbone, cut toward the tail and remove the fillet. Repeat on the other side so you have 2 fillets.

Cajun-style mackerel

This recipe is also referred to as blackened and can be done with Cajun spice. Mackerel is a well-known fish but not very popular and I don't know why: it's delicious and, as a bonus, it's good for you—it's full of omega oils.

SERVES: 4

Preparation time: 10 minutes
Cooking time: 8 minutes

2 tsp paprika
1½ tsp salt
½ tsp onion powder
½ tsp garlic powder
½ tsp white pepper
½ tsp black pepper
½ tsp dried dill
½ tsp dried oregano
2 large mackerel (1lb 2oz each),
    cleaned and filleted
½ cup butter
fresh oregano sprigs
lemon slices
roasted leeks to serve (optional)

method

1 Mix together the paprika, salt, onion powder, garlic powder, white and black pepper, and dried dill and oregano in a small bowl. Sprinkle this spice mixture over each fillet until well coated.

2 Heat half the butter in a heavy-based skillet until very hot, add 2 of the fish fillets, and cook over a medium heat for about 2 minutes on each side. Remove immediately, cover, and keep warm. Add the remaining butter to the pan and cook the other fillets.

3 Transfer the fish to serving plates and garnish with oregano sprigs and lemon slices. Serve with the remaining butter from the pan poured around and accompanied by roasted leeks, if desired.

Alternative fish:
red snapper, tuna, salmon
(make sure they are thick cuts)

CLEANING AND FILLETING SALMON

1 Using the back of a knife and working from the tail to the head, scrape the fish to remove all the scales. Wash the fish under cold water.

2 Using a sharp knife, lift the gill and make a diagonal cut behind through to the backbone.

3 Keeping the knife as close to the backbone as possible, cut toward the tail, lifting the fillet as you go.

4 Run your fingers down the fillet and, using a pair of tweezers or pliers, remove the pin bones all down the fillet.

SALMON PARCEL

1 With a sharp knife, make a horizontal incision in the center of the steak. Cut across to form a pocket in the middle of the steak.

2 Carefully open up the pocket in the steak with your fingers, ready to insert the stuffing.

Salmon stuffed with crab and spinach with dill sauce

This dish is incredibly popular with my customers. It's a very easy recipe that looks fantastic on the plate, so if you want to impress your friends, give this a try.

SERVES: 4

Preparation time: 15 minutes
Cooking time: 12 minutes

4 salmon fillets (6–7oz each)
3½oz fresh crab meat
5 cups fresh spinach, sautéed and
   finely chopped
1 garlic clove, finely chopped
2 cups whole milk
1 tsp soy sauce
¾ cup fresh dill, chopped
lightly steamed snow peas to serve
   (optional)
dill sprigs to garnish

Alternative fish:
salmon trout, halibut, turbot

method

1 Preheat the oven to 350°F.

2 Using a sharp knife, cut a small pocket into the middle of each salmon fillet. In a bowl, mix together the crab meat, spinach, and garlic and stuff into each salmon fillet.

3 Place a large piece of aluminum foil in a roasting pan so that the edges come up the sides of the pan. Place all the fillets in the center of the foil, leaving ½ inch between each one.

4 In a jug, stir together the milk, soy sauce, and dill. Pour over the salmon fillets. Fold over the edges of the foil to enclose the fish and pinch together at the top to form a parcel. Cook in the oven for 10–12 minutes. Be careful not to overcook the salmon: it should be pink on the inside.

5 Serve the salmon hot, on a bed of snow peas if desired, with a little of the sauce on top. Garnish with fresh dill sprigs.

Swordfish paillard on Caesar salad

The firm flesh of swordfish lends itself brilliantly to this simple dish. In my mind, this is one of the best recipes in the book and my customers at Zilli Fish seem to agree!

Alternative fish:
tuna, monkfish

SERVES: 4

Preparation time: 15 minutes plus
  30 minutes marinating time
Cooking time: 12 minutes

4 swordfish steaks (6–7oz each)
3 Tbsp extra virgin olive oil
juice of ½ lemon
1 tsp sea salt
2 baby romaine lettuce, washed and
  leaves separated
1½ cups herb croutons
⅔ cup grated Parmesan
½ cup shaved Parmesan

Caesar dressing
1 egg
2 garlic cloves
3–4 fresh anchovy fillets
  (if canned, use only 2)
2 Tbsp lemon juice
½ cup extra virgin
  olive oil

method

1 Marinate the swordfish in the olive oil, lemon juice, and sea salt for at least half an hour.

2 Make the Caesar dressing by blending in a food processor the egg, garlic, anchovies, and lemon juice. Then, in a steady stream, as if you were making mayonnaise, add the olive oil until the mixture thickens. Store in the refrigerator (for a maximum of 2 days) until ready to use.

3 Using some of the fish marinade, cook the swordfish in a grill pan for 5–6 minutes on each side (depending on the thickness of the steak.) The fish should be cooked but not cooked through, as it will continue to cook while on the plate.

4 In a bowl, mix together the lettuce, croutons, grated Parmesan, and Caesar dressing. Combine well so that the dressing is evenly distributed.

5 Serve the swordfish on top the Caesar salad with the shaved Parmesan on top of the fish. Drizzle with a little of the marinade to serve.

Salmon with bok choy and soy sauce

If you can buy wild salmon—it has a very short season, only 8 weeks in February/March, and is quite expensive in comparison to farmed—it will be worth it as the flavor is amazing and will make a dish like this one a sure winner.

SERVES: 4

Preparation time: 10 minutes
Cooking time: 1 hour 40 minutes

1 leek, chopped
2 carrots, chopped
½ onion
2 bay leaves
4 black peppercorns
4 salmon fillets (5½–6oz each)
½ lemon
8 bok choy heads, blanched
soy sauce to serve

Alternative fish:
trout, sea bass

method

1 First make the broth that you are going to steam the salmon over. Fill a large pot with boiling water and add the leek, carrots, onion, bay leaves, and peppercorns and boil for 1½ hours until the vegetables are soft.

2 Add the salmon to a steamer above the broth, top with the ½ lemon, cover, and cook for 7–8 minutes. Add the blanched bok choy and cook for a further 1 minute. Remove the bok choy and the salmon and place on plate, season with soy sauce, and serve.

Barbecued salmon with potato salad

This is not only a summer recipe—you could also cook the salmon on a simple grill pan or even roast it. The Cajun spice really brings this dish together.

SERVES: 4

Preparation time: 10 minutes plus
   1 hour marinating time
Cooking time: 8–10 minutes

¼ cup extra virgin olive oil
1 Tbsp Cajun spice
1 tsp ground ginger
1 tsp cayenne pepper
1 Tbsp soy sauce
salt and freshly ground black pepper
4 salmon steaks (9oz each)
1lb 2oz new potatoes, boiled
2 eggs, hard boiled
1 small red onion, finely chopped
3 Tbsp chopped parsely
6 tablepoons mayonnaise

method

1 Mix together the oil, Cajun spice, ginger, cayenne, soy sauce, and black pepper in a bowl. Place the salmon in a shallow dish and pour this marinade over. Cover and leave in the refrigerator for 1 hour, turning occasionally.

2 Cut the potatoes in half, roughly chop the eggs, and mix together with the red onion, parsley, and mayonnaise. Season to taste and leave in the refrigerator until ready to use.

3 Heat the barbecue. Remove the salmon steaks from the marinade and place them on the grill. Cook for 3–4 minutes, basting with marinade. Turn over and repeat on the other side.

4 Remove and serve with the potato salad.

Alternative fish:
cod, tuna, swordfish

CUTTING SALMON STEAKS

1 Hold the salmon firmly at the tail end and, with a sharp knife, slice through the fish in one movement. Cut steaks about 1½ inches thick.

Sea trout and noodle salad

Any trout can be used for this recipe. I chose sea trout because the color of the fish looks great on the plate with the noodles. For anyone on a budget, trout is the way forward—and it is as healthy as mackerel or sardines.

SERVES: 4

Preparation time: 10 minutes plus
   45 minutes marinating time
Cooking time: 8 minutes

4 sea trout fillets (7oz each)
2 Tbsp soy sauce
2 Tbsp sake
¼ cup mirin
1 tsp soft brown sugar
2 tsp grated fresh gingerroot
3 garlic cloves
2 Tbsp peanut oil
8oz noodles, cooked
1 cup bean sprouts
2 Tbsp toasted seasame seeds
1 Tbsp chopped cilantro

method

1 Place the trout fillets in a shallow dish. Mix together the soy sauce, sake, mirin, sugar, ginger, and 1 crushed garlic clove. Pour this over the trout, making sure the fish is well coated by turning it in the marinade. Cover with plastic wrap and leave in the refrigerator to marinate for at least 45 minutes.

3 Preheat the broiler. Remove the trout from the dish, reserving the marinade, and place it on a baking sheet. Cook under the broiler for 2–3 minutes (without turning it).

4 Heat the oil in a large heavy skillet. Slice the 2 remaining cloves of garlic and add to the pan; cook until brown but do not allow to burn. Add the noodles and the marinade and cook for 3–4 minutes, stirring constantly. The marinade will reduce and coat the noodles in a syrupy glaze.

5 Add the bean sprouts and remove from the heat. Toss the noodles and transfer to a serving dish, top with the sea trout, and sprinkle with sesame seeds and cilantro before serving.

Alternative fish:
rainbow trout, salmon, swordfish

Right: Sea trout and noodle salad

1 Take several sheets of newspaper and dip them into a bowl of water. Make sure that you wet the whole paper thoroughly.

2 Carefully lay the newspaper on a board and place the fish on top. Lift one side of the paper and roll the fish up.

3 Place on a barbecue and cook. The paper will not burn but rather become hard; turn once. Gently start to open the parcel.

4 When you pull the paper away from the fish, the skin will come off with it. Do not eat the skin because of the dye from the paper.

Trout wrapped in newspaper

When I visited my friend at his house in Italy and saw a newspaper parcel on the barbecue, I thought I was seeing things. He told me about this recipe and I couldn't resist including it in this book. Don't be worried about the paper catching fire—it won't. Rather, it turns into a hard shell-like casing, which adds a smoky flavor to the fish.

SERVES: 4

Preparation time: 15 minutes
Cooking time: 20 minutes

4 trout (1lb each), cleaned
4 sprigs fresh thyme
2 garlic cloves, sliced in half
1 Tbsp extra virgin olive oil
3 Tbsp lemon juice
salt and freshly ground black pepper
newspaper
chopped parsley
lemon wedges to serve
arugula and spinach salad with olive
    oil and balsamic vinegar dressing
    to serve

method

1 Stuff each trout with a sprig of thyme and half a clove of garlic. Brush with olive oil and then sprinkle with lemon juice. Season with salt and pepper.

2 Take the newspaper and wet it, then wrap each fish individually. Place on a barbecue and cook for 20 minutes, turning the parcels occasionally.

3 Remove from the grill and pull the paper off the fish; the skin will come off with the paper leaving you with just the flesh. Sprinkle with chopped parsely and serve with lemon wedges and an arugula and spinach salad with extra virgin olive oil and balsamic vinegar.

Alternative fish:
sea bass, snapper, salmon

Baked stuffed sardines

I love stuffed sardines and tend to eat them every time I am in Italy. Be careful not to over stuff the sardines, as not only will the fish split but they will also take a lot longer to cook.

Alternative fish:
herring, mackerel, trout

SERVES: 4

Preparation time: 25 minutes
Cooking time: 30 minutes

1 Tbsp olive oil
1 onion, finely chopped
1 garlic clove, crushed
1½ cups fresh breadcrumbs
1 Tbsp wholegrain mustard
2 Tbsp chopped parsley
1 egg yolk
2 Tbsp ricotta cheese
juice of 3 lemons and zest of 1
salt and freshly ground black pepper
12 fresh sardines, cleaned and
    boned (see pages 80–1)
lemon wedges and parsley to serve

method

1 Heat the oil and pan-fry the onions and garlic over a low heat until softened—approximately 5 minutes. Remove the garlic clove. Preheat the oven to 350°F.

2 Remove the pan from the heat and stir in the breadcrumbs, mustard, chopped parsley, egg yolk, and ricotta cheese. Stir in the juice of 2 lemons and season to taste.

3 Using a teaspoon, fill the sardines with the stuffing. Lay a large piece of aluminum foil in an ovenproof dish and place the sardines on top. Add the remaining lemon juice and zest, fold the edges of the foil over, and pinch to seal. Bake for 30 minutes.

Rosemary tuna kabobs

Rosemary is definitely my favorite herb to have with fish and these skewers are great as the herb flavors the fish while cooking and releases a wonderful smell.

Alternative:
scallops, swordfish, monkfish

SERVES: 4

Preparation time: 15 minutes
Cooking time: 5 minutes

8 long stems of rosemary, some of
    the stem leaves removed
2¼lb tuna, cut into 1½-inch chunks
8 cherry tomatoes
2 Tbsp extra virgin olive oil
cracked black pepper
arugula to serve (optional)

Houmous
1 large eggplant, roasted
1 cup chickpeas
½ cup sundried tomatoes
2 garlic cloves
juice of 1 lemon
½ cup olive oil
salt and freshly ground
    black pepper

method

1 Thread the rosemary skewers through the tuna chunks and cherry tomatoes to make 8 kabobs, then roll the kabobs in the olive oil and cracked black pepper.

2 Scoop the flesh from the center of the eggplant and discard the skin. Place the eggplant, chickpeas, sundried tomatoes, garlic, lemon juice, and olive oil into a blender and process until smooth. Season to taste.

3 Heat the barbecue and cook the kabobs for 4 minutes, turning to ensure that each side is browning. Remove and serve with the houmous and some arugula, if desired. The tuna should still be pink in the middle.

Trout with apples, cider, and cream

Not being a great drinker of cider—alcoholic apple juice really—I thought I would try this one day with a bottle of cider someone had given me. It worked brilliantly!

SERVES: 4

Preparation time: 10 minutes plus
   1 hour marinating time
Cooking time: 15 minutes

⅓ cup olive oil
⅔ cup lemon juice
3 garlic cloves, crushed
2 Tbsp chopped parsley
3 Tbsp finely chopped chives
4 trout fillets (7oz each)
⅓ cup hard cider
3 Tbsp butter
2 Tbsp cream
1 cooking apple, cut
   into thin slices

method

1 Mix together the oil, lemon juice, garlic, parsley, and chives. Place the fillets in this marinade and leave in the refrigerator for at least 1 hour. Preheat the oven to 325°F.

2 Meanwhile simmer the cider until reduced by half. Reduce the heat and add the butter and cream, stirring to combine until the butter has melted.

3 Pan-fry the trout for 3 minutes on each side. Transfer the fish to a serving dish and bake in the preheated oven for 10 minutes.

4 Add the apple slices to the skillet, sprinkle with some brown sugar, and cook over a high heat for about 10 minutes until they are golden brown. Remove apples and add sauce to pan.

5 Serve the trout with the sauce poured over and apple slices laid on top of the fish.

Alternative fish:
salmon, parrot fish, butterfish

CLEANING AND BONING SARDINES

1 This method for cleaning and boning sardines can also be used for anchovies and small herrings or mackerel.

2 Holding the fish by the tail, run the back of a knife down the sides of the fish to remove any scales.

3 Remove all the fins from the sardine using a pair of scissors.

4 Using a pair of scissors, make an incision in the belly near the tail and cut toward the head.

Sardines with spaghetti Sicilian style

Sardines, like mackerel, are very good for you. Both are also very versatile and can be cooked in a variety of ways. As I'm Italian, this method is obviously one of my favorites.

SERVES: 4

Preparation time: 15 minutes
Cooking time: 15 minutes

12 fresh sardines, cleaned and boned
1 cup olive oil
1 onion, chopped
½ cup fresh dill, chopped
½ cup toasted pine nuts
2 Tbsp raisins, soaked
salt and freshly ground black pepper
1lb spaghetti
½ cup flour

method

1 Rinse the sardines under water and pat them dry. Open them out flat and cut in half lengthwise.

2 Heat 2 tablespoons of the oil in a heavy skillet, add the onion, and cook over a medium heat for 5–8 minutes, stirring occasionally, until golden. Lower the heat, add the dill, and continue cooking for a further 2 minutes. Stir in the pine nuts and raisins, season to taste with salt and pepper, and set aside (keeping it warm).

3 Bring a pan of salted water to a boil and add the spaghetti. Cook for the time stated on the packet instructions. It should be al dente—slightly firm to the bite.

4 Meanwhile, heat the remaining oil in a pan. Dust the sardines with flour, shaking off any excess. Add the sardines to the oil and sauté for 2–3 minutes. Drain on paper towels.

5 Drain the spaghetti and return it to the pan. Add the onion mixture and toss well. Transfer the spaghetti to a large serving plate and arrange the sardines on top. Serve immediately.

Alternative fish:
anchovies, small herrings

5 Pull out the sardine's innards and discard.

6 Cut off the head of the sardine and discard. Wash the sardine thoroughly under cold water.

7 Place the sardine on a flat board, skin side up, and push the backbone down with your fingers until the fish is almost flat against the board.

8 Turn the sardine over and pull out the backbone.

Fried whitebait with paprika

Some people are very funny about this classic whitebait dish as you eat the whole fish, bones and all. I've seen some customers trying to fillet whitebait, but this is a waste of time. Not only will you end up with hardly any meat, but the best flavor is in the bones.

SERVES: 4

Preparation time: 5 minutes plus
   1 hour marinating time
Cooking time: 3 minutes

1lb 2oz whitebait
2 tsp sea salt
2 Tbsp all-purpose flour
1 Tbsp paprika
2 tsp finely chopped parsley
salt and freshly ground black pepper
vegetable oil for frying
lemon wedges, tartare sauce, and
   chopped parsley to serve
   (optional)

method

1 Combine the whitebait and sea salt in a dish, mix well, and refrigerate for 1 hour.

2 Sift the flour and paprika into a bowl, add the parsley, and season with salt and pepper.

3 Heat the vegetable oil in either a deep-fat fryer or a large saucepan. When it is hot enough, a pinch of flour dropped into it will sizzle immediately.

4 Toss some of the whitebait in the flour and paprika, then shake off excess flour and deep-fry in 2 batches for 2–3 minutes each batch until a pale gold color. Drain onto paper towels.

5 Serve immediately, with lemon wedges and tartare sauce and sprinkled with more chopped parsley if desired.

Alternative fish:
sprats, anchovies

Boneless herring dipped in egg and fried in garlic butter

I love eggy pan-fried fish as it always gives a lovely golden color to the dish. If you are pan-frying any fish in breadcrumbs or another coating, make sure you flour the fish first. This will ensure the coatings stick to the fish.

SERVES: 4

Preparation time: 10 minutes
Cooking time: 8 minutes

plain flour for coating
salt and freshly ground black pepper
5 Tbsp unsalted butter
2 Tbsp finely chopped garlic
2 eggs, whisked
8 herring fillets

method

1 Season the flour with the salt and pepper and place in a shallow dish. In a large skillet, heat the butter. Add the garlic and cook over a medium heat for 2 minutes. Make sure you do not burn the garlic as this will ruin the flavor.

2 Place the beaten eggs into a shallow dish. Dip the herrings in the flour, then into the egg. Sauté the coated fish in the garlic butter for 8 minutes, turning occasionally.

3 Serve on a plate with the remaining garlic butter poured over.

Alternative fish:
sardines, mackerel

Right: Fried whitebait with paprika

Green onion pancakes with gravlax

Salmon is such a versatile fish and gravlax makes an expensive but impressive dish to prepare for friends. You can, of course, buy ready-made gravlax, but I think making it yourself is what makes this dish special. If you are using smoked salmon or haddock, just lay the slices on top of the pancake.

SERVES: 4

Preparation time: 20 minutes plus
   pancake mix to rest overnight
Cooking time: 8 minutes

¾ cup butter
2 eggs
1 cup milk
1 cup all-purpose flour
2½ tsp baking powder
½ tsp salt
¼ cup chopped green onions
juice of 2 lemons
salt and freshly ground black pepper
1 cucumber
3 cups aragula
16 slices gravlax

method

1 Melt 3 tablespoons of butter and allow to cool. Place in a bowl with eggs and milk and whisk until combined. Sift the flour, baking powder, and salt into a bowl, make a well in the center, and gradually add the egg mix, beating until the batter is smooth. Leave in the refrigerator overnight.

2 Heat a non-stick skillet and ladle 4 tablespoons of batter into the pan. You should be able to make 2 pancakes at the same time. Sprinkle each pancake with 1 tablespoon of chopped green onions and cook for about 2 minutes, or until bubbles begin to appear on the surface. Turn pancakes over and cook the other side. Keep the pancakes warm while cooking remaining ones.

3 Make lemon butter by heating the lemon juice and whisking in the remaining butter, a bit at a time, until melted. Season with salt and pepper. Cut cucumber into ribbons with a vegetable peeler.

4 Place a pancake on each plate and top with aragula, 4 slices of gravlax, and a pile of cucumber ribbons. Spoon lemon butter around the pancake and serve.

Alternative fish:
smoked salmon, haddock

Marinated anchovies

I hold monthly masterclasses in my restaurants and this is one of the dishes I teach: it is the most requested recipe of the course. If the anchovies are covered in oil, you can keep them in the refrigerator for up to 3 weeks.

SERVES: 2

Preparation time: 10 minutes plus
   15 hours (total) marinating time

1 bottle white wine vinegar
1 glass white wine
juice of 3 lemons
5 Tbsp sea salt
4 bay leaves
2 sprigs thyme
8 garlic cloves
12 fresh anchovies, boned
2 chilies, finely chopped
2 Tbsp chopped parsley
⅓ cup extra virgin olive oil

method

1 In a bowl, mix together white wine vinegar, white wine, lemon juice, sea salt, bay leaves, thyme, and 5 whole garlic cloves. Place the anchovies in a flat dish and pour over this marinade. Leave to marinate in a cool place for at least 12 hours.

2 Remove anchovies from the marinade and dip into a bowl of water. Pat dry with paper towels and place on a shallow plate.

3 Finely chop remaining garlic cloves and sprinkle over the anchovies with the chopped chili and parsley. Pour olive oil over, making sure all the fish are covered. Marinate for at least 3 hours before serving.

Alternative fish:
baby sardines, sprats

*Right: Green onion pancake
with gravlax*

MAKING GRAVLAX

1 Place the salmon skin side down on a plate and pat crushed sea salt and crushed black peppercorns onto the top. Pour brandy over.

2 Cover the top with chopped dill. Cover with plastic wrap and place a heavy object on top of the fish. Place in the refrigerator overnight.

3 Remove from the refrigerator and carefully lift out the salmon. Using a sharp knife, gently remove the skin from the salmon.

4 Using a very sharp knife, slice the salmon lengthwise as thinly as you like.

Seared tuna with sticky rice, wasabi, and soy sauce

This very lightly cooked recipe is fantastic! I don't understand people eating well-done tuna—you might as well eat canned tuna. If you need to watch your weight, leave out the rice and serve with arugula and Parmesan salad.

SERVES: 4

Preparation time: 10 minutes
Cooking time: 3 minutes

¼ cup olive oil
½ tsp salt
3 Tbsp freshly cracked black pepper
2 tsp paprika
small fillet of tuna (1lb 5oz)
2 cups sticky rice, cooked
soy sauce and wasabi to serve

Alternative fish:
salmon, swordfish,
sea bass

method

1 Heat a skillet and add the oil. In a bowl mix together the salt, pepper, and paprika and use to season the tuna fillet. Place the tuna in the pan of hot oil and sear for 1 minute on each side. Remove from the pan and leave to cool.

2 Divide the sticky rice between 4 teacups, pat down, then turn out onto 4 plates. Slice the tuna very thinly and place over the rice. Serve with the soy sauce and wasabi.

Salmon carpaccio with pine nuts and soy sauce

Carpaccio, which translates as "raw," is normally associated with beef, but adapting it for fish is great too. As with sushi and sashimi, you must make sure that you use only fish that is extremely fresh, so find a good fish store or large market.

1 Holding the blade of a very sharp knife nearly horizontal to the side of salmon, ~~slice~~ ~~very~~ thinly. You should be ~~~~ ~~the~~ blade through

SERVES: 4

Preparation time: 40 minutes

1lb 2oz sushi-grade salmon
1 Tbsp extra virgin olive oil
1 Tbsp lime juice
2 Tbsp soy sauce
salt and freshly ground black pepper
1 fennel bulb, thinly sliced
3 Tbsp pine nuts, toasted
 and crushed
½ medium cucumber, thinly sliced
2 Tbsp finely chopped green onions
grated zest of 1 lime

method

1 Wrap the salmon in plastic wrap and freeze for 20–30 minutes until it is partly frozen to make it easier to slice.

2 Remove the salmon and unwrap. Using a sharp knife or a slicer cut into thin slices across the grain.

3 To make the dressing, whisk together the olive oil, lime juice, and soy sauce and season to taste.

4 Place the fennel in the center of each serving plate and arrange salmon slices around the outside. Scatter crushed pine nuts, cucumber, green onions, and lime zest over the salmon and then drizzle with some of the dressing. Leave in the refrigerator for 1 hour before serving with small bowls of remaining dressing.

Alternative fish:
tuna, swordfish, scallops

Spicy mackerel pâté

Fish pâté used to be extremely popular and I think it is time we brought it back into favor. Try this recipe and see if you agree. It also makes a great snack for your kids when they get home from school and will stop them from filling up with chips.

SERVES: 4

Preparation time: 15 minutes plus
    4 hours chilling time

4 smoked, peppered mackerel fillets
    (6oz each), skinned and flaked
1 cup ricotta cheese
2 garlic cloves, finely chopped
juice of 1 lemon
2 Tbsp chopped chives
1 Tbsp Worcestershire sauce
salt and cayenne pepper to taste
chopped chives and toasted brown
    bread to serve

method

1 Place the smoked mackerel, ricotta cheese, garlic, lemon juice, and chives in a food processor and blend until the mixture is fairly smooth, then add the Worcestershire sauce and salt and cayenne pepper to taste. Blend for a further 1 minute to ensure it is well mixed.

2 Spoon the pâté into a buttered dish, cover with plastic wrap, and chill in the refrigerator for 4 hours.

3 Garnish with some more chives and serve with toasted brown bread.

Alternative fish:
haddock, sardines

Smoked eel, endive, and radicchio salad

I think that you either love eel or hate it—there's no in-between with this fish. I like to make this salad when it is a beautiful summer's day—it's lovely and crisp.

SERVES: 4

Preparation time: 15 minutes

1lb smoked eel fillets, skinned
2 endive heads
4 radicchio leaves
2 Tbsp golden raisins
4 green onions, sliced

Dressing
juice of 1 orange and zest of ½
juice of 1 lime and zest of ½
1 tsp sugar
1 tsp wholegrain mustard
6 Tbsp olive oil
2 Tbsp chopped parsley
salt and freshly ground black pepper

method

1 Cut the eel into strips about 1½ inches wide.

2 To make the dressing, place the orange juice in a pan and add the orange and lime zests and the sugar. Bring to a boil, then lower the heat and reduce by half. Leave to cool completely.

3 Whisk together the lime juice, mustard, and olive oil, then add the reduced orange juice. Stir in the parsley and season to taste.

4 Arrange the endive and radicchio leaves on 4 plates and top with eel strips. Scatter over the golden raisins and green onions, then drizzle over dressing.

Alternative fish:
smoked trout

Right: Smoked eel, endive, and radicchio salad

Baby smoked herring with beets and soured cream

My fish supplier delivered me smoked herring by mistake one day so I concocted this great salad. It is now a firm favorite and has become a regular fixture on the Salad Bar at Zilli Café.

SERVES: 4

Preparation time: 10 minutes

9oz smoked baby herrings, cut into slices
1 small cooking apple, cored, peeled, and diced
6 gherkins, diced
1 tsp refined sugar
1 tsp white wine vinegar
⅔ cup soured cream
1 cooked beet, diced
1 red leaf lettuce
1 green leaf lettuce
½ red onion, sliced

method

1 Place the herrings, apple, gherkins, sugar, and vinegar into a bowl and mix well together. Add the soured cream and combine, then gently fold in the diced beets. Place in the refrigerator to chill.

2 Serve on the red and green leaf lettuce and garnish with the red onion slices.

Alternative fish:
smoked sardines

Smoked trout and potato salad

Trout, hot- or cold-smoked or fresh or otherwise, is a great fish. My favorite is salmon or sea trout as I find river trout too strong. This simple recipe came to me years ago for salmon but it is just as delicious made with trout.

SERVES: 4

Preparation time: 20 minutes
Cooking time: 10–15 minutes

½ cup extra virgin olive oil
3 Tbsp lemon juice
1 Tbsp red wine vinegar
1 garlic clove crushed with sea salt
freshly ground black pepper
2 Tbsp chopped mint
2 Tbsp chopped parsley
2 Tbsp finely chopped green onions
1 red bell pepper, seeded and thinly
    sliced
1 stalk celery, sliced
1 Tbsp capers
1lb 2oz unpeeled waxy potatoes
9oz cold-smoked rainbow trout, skin
    and bones removed

Lemon mayonnaise
1 egg yolk
zest of 1 lemon
3 Tbsp lemon juice
sea salt and freshly ground black
    pepper
½ cup mild oil

Alternative fish:
smoked mackerel

method

1 To make the mayonnaise, place the egg yolk, lemon zest and juice, and salt and pepper to taste in a bowl or food processor and whisk until combined. Add the oil drop by drop, whisking constantly. When it starts to thicken, add the oil in a steady stream until fully combined. If mayonnaise is too thick, add a tablespoon of warm water. Store in the refrigerator.

2 Place the olive oil, lemon juice, vinegar, garlic, salt, and pepper in a bowl and whisk. Stir in mint, parsley, green onions, bell pepper, celery, and capers.

3 Cook the potatoes in salted water until tender. Drain and allow to cool for a few minutes, or until you can handle them, before peeling and slicing them.

4 Add the potatoes to the dressing while they are still warm and stir gently to combine.

5 Divide the potato salad between 4 plates and top each with some smoked trout. Drizzle with lemon mayonnaise to serve.

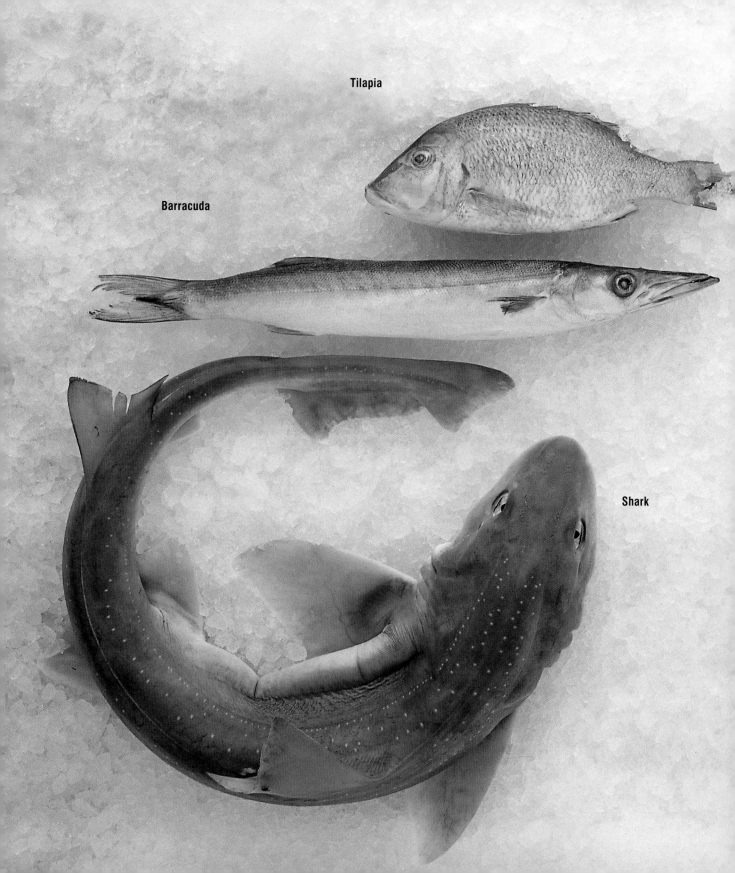

Tilapia

Barracuda

Shark

Exotic Fish

Butterfish

Red emperor

Parrot fish

Barramundi

Yellowtail snapper

Exotic Fish

When I first came to the UK, the likelihood of finding any of these fish was very rare. Now, thanks to improved storing of fish and importing, many more exotic fish varieties can be found in the USA also, in good markets or supermarkets. This is a huge section of fish and it would be impossible for me to name them all, so I have tried to choose those that are fairly easily available all over the world. (Don't be confused by my list of exotic fish: people living in other countries—Australia, for example—will think of barramundi and barracuda as common fare and will probably consider some of the fish I have included in other chapters more exotic.) Some exotic fish that you can buy in the USA will be frozen. When the fish are caught, they are immediately put in the freezer on the boats before being exported and the quality of these "frozen as fresh" fish is surprisingly good. Don't be put off by the fact that you are not acquainted with these fish: while they might look different to the fish that you are used to, they are nonetheless very tasty and can often be prepared, cooked, and eaten in much the same way as any more well-known fish.

BARRACUDA genus *Sphyraena*
Barracudas are usually found in warm, tropical regions. They are swift and powerful, small scaled, and slender in form, with two well-separated dorsal fins, a jutting lower jaw, and a large mouth with many sharp, large teeth. Size varies from rather small to as large as 4–6 feet in the great barracuda of the Atlantic, Caribbean, and the Pacific. They are good, fighting sporting fishes, and the smaller ones make good eating. Barracudas are bold, inquisitive, and fearsome fish, which may be dangerous to humans. (The great barracuda is known to have been involved in attacks on swimmers.) Barracuda is quite an oily fish, so avoid cooking it with butter or cream.

BARRAMUNDI *Lates calcarifer*
This fish has gained a reputation of being one of Australia's finest eating fish. Barramundi are excellent table fish with relatively few bones and a firm, white, fine-grained flesh with a delicate flavor that can be prepared in a number of ways. They resemble giant perch and can grow to a large size, sometimes weighing more than 44lb, though fish of 11–13lb are more usual.

BUTTERFISH *Pampus argenteus*
Butterfish, known as pomfret in the UK, are normally about 8 inches long. The butterfish's back is a leaden bluish color, its sides are paler, and it has a silvery belly. The body is thin and deep with almost no scales and resembles that of a flat fish. Butterfish look like angel fish and although they don't have much flesh, what they do have is lovely with a strong, firm, texture. Butterfish is becoming increasingly popular in the USA and is one of few fish species worldwide deemed to be under-exploited.

MAHI MAHI *Coryphaenidae hippurus*
Also known as dolphin fish and dorado, the mahi mahi tapers sharply from head to tail and is a bright, greeny blue fish with yellow down its sides. When stressed, it flashes neon purple. Mahi mahi has a wonderfully tender white flesh and when cooked has a rich succulent flavor, which lends itself to any recipe.

MARLIN genus *Makaira*
There are two main types of marlin—blue and white—and both are a popular catch with sports fishermen. Marlin is normally sold in steaks and is similar to swordfish and tuna with flesh that is a slightly darker white color than that of swordfish. Although it makes good eating, marlin lacks the delicate flavor of swordfish.

PARROT FISH family Scaridae
It always seems a pity to eat this beautiful-looking fish, but when you combine parrot fish with strong flavors they make for great eating. Parrot fish are bony, marine fish whose teeth have fused to form an extremely hard beak, which enables them to bite off pieces of coral. This, with seaweed and molluscs, forms their principal food. All parrot fish are brilliantly colored and some may grow to as large as 40 inches in length, although they are generally smaller than this.

RED EMPEROR *Lutjanus sebae*
Red emperors belong to the tropical snapper and sea perch family and are salmon pink to red in color with pink fins tipped with bright crimson and three distinctive darker red bands. They are normally fished in the Australian tropical seas and can weigh more than 40lb, although an average fish is usually around 4½–15½lb. Red emperor has delicate white flesh and makes excellent eating.

SHARK genus *Alopias* and others
Shark have a cartilaginous skeleton and lack the sort of small bones that put some people off eating fish. Like skate, they tend to have an ammonia smell, but this disappears with cooking. If however, you are given a cooked piece of shark and it still smells of ammonia, it is old and should be sent back to the kitchen.

TILAPIA genus *Tilapia*
Although they are found mainly in tropical seas, tilapia can live in fresh water or salt water. Most fresh tilapia come from Columbia and Costa Rica, while frozen tilapia is imported from the Far East. Tilapia are now available all year round in the USA where they are farmed. Tilapia have a huge range of colors, from gray to bright red. The meat is white and firm, but is bland, so lends itself to spicy dishes.

YELLOWTAIL SNAPPER *Ocyurus chrysurus*
Yellowtail snappers are easily distinguished by the yellow stripes down the side of their body and the yellow spots on their back. They feed on small fish and normally weigh around 3–5lb. They are very popular in the Caribbean, where they are found in large numbers.

Butterfish with tamarind and chili sauce

While this is an unusual fish in both looks and taste, it is perfect for the barbecue. With the additional strong flavors of tamarind and chili, this is a dish well worth making.

SERVES: 4

Preparation time: 10 minutes
Cooking time: 10 minutes

4 butterfish (9oz each), cleaned
6 green onions, chopped
3 Tbsp soy sauce
12 cherry tomatoes, halved
2 Tbsp chopped fresh cilantro

Sauce

2oz tamarind pulp
7 Tbsp boiling water
2 shallots, coarsely chopped
1 stalk lemongrass, peeled and chopped
1 fresh red chili, seeded and chopped
½ tsp finely chopped fresh gingerroot
1 tsp brown sugar
3 Tbsp nam pla (fish sauce)

method

1 Slash the butterfish 3 times on each side with a sharp knife and place in a shallow dish.

2 Fill the slashes with green onions and pour over the soy sauce. Turn the fish to coat both sides in the soy sauce. Set aside.

3 To make the sauce, put the tamarind in a bowl and add the boiling water. Mash until soft, then tip into a blender and process. Stir in the shallots, lemongrass, chili, ginger, sugar, and fish sauce.

4 Cook the fish on the barbecue with some cherry tomatoes for about 5 minutes on each side, until the skin is crispy and the fish is cooked. Alternatively, heat some oil in a skillet and cook the fish for about 3 minutes on each side. Spoon over sauce, sprinkle with cilantro, and serve.

Alternative fish:
bream, mullet

CLEANING AND SCALING SNAPPER

1 Holding on to the tail, drag a sharp knife along the fish to remove scales. If you are nervous about cutting the fish, use the back of the knife.

2 Using a sharp pair of scissors, cut off all the fins, then cut open the belly of the fish from the tail to the head.

3 Using your fingers, reach inside the cavity of the fish and pull out and discard all the guts. Rinse the fish under cold water.

Spicy baked yellowtail snapper with pine nuts

If you can't find a whole fish then use fillets, but roast the fillet for only half the time stated for a whole fish. Pine nuts work particularly well with fish, but if you are unfortunate enough to be allergic to nuts, you can omit them.

SERVES: 4

Preparation time: 10 minutes plus 2 hours marinating time
Cooking time: 35 minutes

13oz yellowtail snapper, cleaned and scaled
½ tsp salt
juice of 2 lemons
¼ cup extra virgin olive oil
2 onions, sliced
4 garlic cloves, chopped
1 green bell pepper, seeded and diced
2 fresh green chilies, seeded and finely chopped
½ tsp ground turmeric
½ tsp curry powder
½ tsp ground cumin
½ cup Italian-style strained tomatoes
5 fresh tomatoes, peeled and chopped
¼ cup chopped fresh cilantro
½ cup pine nuts, toasted

method

1 Using a fork, prick the fish all over then rub with salt. Place on a roasting pan and sprinkle lemon juice all over. Leave to marinate for 2 hours.

2 Preheat the oven to 350°F. Heat the oil in a pan and add the onions and half the garlic and cook until softened. Add the bell pepper, chilies, turmeric, curry powder, and cumin to the pan and cook gently for 2–3 minutes. Stir in the tomatoes (strained and chopped) and cilantro.

3 Sprinkle half the pine nuts over the base of an ovenproof dish and top with half the sauce. Add the fish and its marinade, sprinkle remaining garlic over, and then top with the remaining sauce and pine nuts. Cover with aluminum foil and bake in the oven for 30 minutes.

Alternative fish:
red snapper, red bream

Parrot fish with red curry paste

Curry tends to marry well with shellfish but when I tried it with this kind of fish it was equally successful. Green curry paste will not work, however, as the flavor of the curry, rather than adding to the fish, will overwhelm it.

SERVES: 6

Preparation time: 10 minutes
Cooking time: 30 minutes

1 small grapefruit
1 blood orange
1 lemon
1 parrot fish (3lb), cleaned and
   scaled
salt and freshly ground black pepper
2 Tbsp Thai red curry paste
5 shallots, halved
3 Tbsp olive oil
¼ cup white wine
3 Tbsp butter, melted

Alternative fish:
bream, sea bass

method

1 Preheat the oven to 375°F. Using a vegetable peeler, remove the rind from the grapefruit, blood orange, and lemon and cut into strips. Peel and discard the white pith from the fruits. Cut the grapefruit and blood orange into segments, reserving the juice, and cut the lemon into thick slices.

2 Season the inside of the fish with salt and pepper and make 3 diagonal slashes in the side of the fish. Fill the inside of the fish with the lemon slices and half of the citrus rinds. Spread the curry paste over the top of the fish making sure to get some in the slashes.

3 Lay the fish in a roasting pan, add the shallot halves and drizzle over 1½ tablespoons of oil. Roast in the oven for about 15 minutes. Remove from the oven, carefully turn the fish and stir the shallots, drizzle with remaining oil, and roast for a further 10–15 minutes until cooked through.

4 Remove the fish from the pan and keep warm. Skim off excess oil and add the wine and fruit juices to the pan. Bring to a boil and stir in remaining rinds. Whisk in the butter and spoon the sauce and shallots around the fish. Serve with the grapefruit and orange segments and lemon slices.

PAN-FRYING WHOLE FISH

1 Insert into the cavity of the fish any herbs or other stuffing ingredients that you wish to use. Sprinkle the fish with sea salt.

2 Place the fish on a plate of seasoned flour and pat flour all over the fish, making sure that you cover it completely.

3 Wrap the tail in foil to prevent it burning. Place the fish in a pan of hot oil and pan-fry over medium heat for 10 minutes on each side.

4 If you wish, add some sauce to the pan just before the fish is cooked. This will ensure that the fish absorbs the sauce flavors.

Tilapia with fruit sauce

I love cooking with fruit, especially mango or papaya, and tilapia cooked whole like this is fantastic. Tilapia comes from the Caribbean but is now being farmed in the USA.

SERVES: 4

Preparation time: 15 minutes plus overnight marinating time
Cooking time: 40 minutes

4 tilapia (12oz each), cleaned
juice of ½ lemon
2 garlic cloves, crushed
½ tsp dried thyme
2 Tbsp chopped green onions
vegetable oil for frying
flour for coating
2 Tbsp peanut oil
1 Tbsp butter
1 onion, finely chopped
3 tomatoes, peeled and finely chopped
1 tsp ground turmeric
¼ cup white wine
1 fresh green chili, seeded and finely chopped
2½ cups fish stock
1 tsp sugar
1 medium under-ripe mango
1 Tbsp chopped fresh parsley

method

1 Place the fish in a bowl and pour the lemon juice over, then rub in the garlic, thyme, and some salt and freshly ground black pepper. Place some of the green onions in each fish and then cover the bowl with plastic wrap and leave overnight.

2 Heat some vegetable oil in a large heavy-based skillet. Coat the fish with flour, making sure you shake off any excess. Pan-fry the fish on both sides over a medium heat for a few minutes until golden brown. Remove from the pan and set to one side.

3 Heat the peanut oil and butter in another pan, add the onion, and cook over a low heat for 4–5 minutes until softened. Stir in the tomatoes, turn up the heat, and cook for a few more minutes.

4 Add the turmeric, white wine, chili, fish stock, and sugar to the pan and stir well. Bring to a boil, then lower the heat, cover, and simmer for 12 minutes.

5 Add the fish to the pan and cook for a further 15 minutes until the fish is cooked through. Peel, pit, and chop the mango, stir it into the sauce, and cook for a further 2 minutes.

6 Serve the fish on a platter with the fruit sauce poured over. Garnish with the chopped parsley and serve immediately, with some minted new potatoes if desired.

Alternative fish:
John Dory, gray mullet, sea bream

Mahi mahi poached in milk with herb sauce

Milk poaching is a great way of cooking that I first used for salmon—it was lovely and moist.
Mahi mahi also tastes wonderful roasted with garlic and rosemary.

SERVES: 4

Preparation time: 10 minutes
Cooking time: 20 minutes

4 mahi mahi fillets (6½oz each)
2 Tbsp lemon juice
½ tsp salt
½ tsp ground black pepper
3 cups milk
½ cup fish stock
1 white onion, chopped
2 tsp chopped fresh thyme
1 Tbsp black peppercorns
1 Tbsp chopped fresh parsley
roasted leeks to serve (optional)

method

1 Place the fish in a shallow dish and rub with the lemon juice and sprinkle with the salt and pepper, set aside to marinate.

2 In a saucepan combine the milk, fish stock, onion, thyme, and peppercorns and bring to a boil. Gently slide in the fish fillets and simmer for 15 minutes. Remove the fish and keep warm.

3 Bring the milk back to a boil and reduce the liquid by three quarters, then add the parsley. Serve the fish covered in the herb sauce, with roasted leeks if desired.

Alternative fish:
salmon, cod

Marlin with black pepper and cream sauce

This is traditionally a sauce that is used with steak, but I tried it one day with fish and really loved it. Use a firm fish as delicate fish will be swamped by the rich sauce.

Alternative fish:
tuna, swordfish

SERVES: 4

Preparation time: 10 minutes plus
   1 hour marinating time
Cooking time: 35 minutes

4 marlin steaks (6oz each)
1 tsp sea salt
2 Tbsp olive oil
1 Tbsp lemon juice
14oz potatoes, peeled and quartered
2 Tbsp butter
1 Tbsp olive oil
pinch saffron strands, melted in
   hot water

Black pepper sauce
olive oil for stir-frying
1 Tbsp chopped onion
2 Tbsp chopped garlic
1 Tbsp sugar
¼ cup cream
2 Tbsp oyster sauce
1 Tbsp soy sauce
2 Tbsp cracked black pepper

method

1 Marinate the marlin in the sea salt, oil, and lemon juice.

2 To make the sauce, stir-fry the onion until it becomes translucent. Stir in the garlic, sugar, cream, oyster sauce, soy sauce, and black pepper. Simmer for 15 minutes over a low heat.

3 Meanwhile, cook the potatoes until soft, remove from the heat, and strain. Add the butter and olive oil and mash. When smooth, add the saffron and, using a spatula, mix until completely incorporated. Keep warm.

4 Pan-fry the marlin in some of the marinade for 7 minutes on each side. Serve with saffron mash and black pepper sauce.

Shark steaks Moroccan style

I created this recipe in the '80s when shark was very cheap, but I still put it on the menu every now and then and it is very popular. It holds special memories for me—I cooked it for my wife Nikki the first time I met her in my restaurant.

SERVES: 4

Preparation time: 15 minutes plus
    2 hours marinating time
Cooking time: 10 minutes

⅔ cup olive oil
1 Tbsp paprika
2 tsp harissa (chili sauce)
2 tsp cumin
2 garlic cloves, crushed
juice of 2 lemons
salt and freshly ground black pepper
3 Tbsp chopped cilantro
2 Tbsp chopped mint
4 shark steaks (6½oz each)
lemon wedges to serve

method

1 In a bowl, mix together the olive oil, paprika, harissa, cumin, garlic, and lemon juice. Season, then stir in the chopped cilantro and mint.

2 Pour the marinade into a non-metallic dish large enough to fit the shark steaks in a single layer. Turn the shark steaks over in the dish to ensure that they are evenly coated with the marinade. Cover the dish with plastic wrap and place in the refrigerator for 2 hours.

3 Heat the broiler to medium-high, then broil the shark steaks for 5 minutes on each side until just cooked, turning the steaks once and basting them several times with the marinade. Serve immediately with lemon wedges.

Alternative fish:
monkfish, swordfish, cod

Braised barramundi with shellfish

Some of you may not be very familiar with this fish. Well neither was I, but I highly recommend it. It is very well known as lungfish in Australia, where you can buy it fresh; in the USA frozen barramundi is often available.

SERVES: 4

Preparation time: 10 minutes
Cooking time: 15 minutes

2 Tbsp olive oil
1 onion, thinly sliced
1 yellow bell pepper, seeded and
    cut into strips
1¾ cups Italian-style strained
    tomatoes
3 Tbsp dry white wine
2 zucchini, sliced
1lb mixed shellfish
12oz skinned barramundi fillets,
    cut into 2-inch chunks
salt and freshly ground black pepper
juice of ½ lemon
2 Tbsp shredded fresh basil
noodles or pasta to serve (optional)

method

1 Heat the oil in a large skillet, add the onion and bell pepper, and stir-fry for 2 minutes until the onion is translucent.

2 Stir the strained tomatoes and the white wine into the pan and bring to a boil. Lower the heat and simmer for 2 minutes.

3 Add the zucchini, mixed shellfish, and barramundi, cover, and cook over a low heat for about 5 minutes, stirring occasionally. Season to taste with salt, pepper, and lemon juice, and simmer for a further 4 minutes, then stir in half the shredded basil.

4 Garnish with remaining basil and serve with noodles or pasta, if desired.

Alternative fish:
cod, salmon, halibut, swordfish, snapper, ocean perch

Left: Shark steaks Moroccan style

Barbecued red emperor with herb relish

This fish is extremely popular in Australia where it is also called the emperor snapper fish. Barbecuing has to be one of the best methods of cooking red emperor or indeed any kind of fish—it's lovely and fresh as well as healthy.

SERVES: 4

Preparation time: 10 minutes plus
    2 hours marinating time
Cooking time: 10 minutes

¼ cup olive oil
2 Tbsp chopped fresh dill
1 Tbsp chopped fresh parsley
1 Tbsp chopped fresh lemon thyme
1 Tbsp fresh lemon juice
1 tsp minced garlic
2 Tbsp finely chopped red onion
2 Tbsp sherry vinegar
4 red emperor fillets (7oz each)
salt and freshly ground black pepper

method

1 Mix together 2 tablespoons of olive oil, the dill, parsley, lemon thyme, lemon juice, garlic, red onion, and sherry vinegar. Set aside for the flavors to combine.

2 Rub the fish fillets with the remaining olive oil and season both sides. Place the fillets on a hot barbecue and cook for 5 minutes on each side.

3 Remove fish from the grill and serve topped with the herb relish.

Alternative fish:
snapper, mullet

Barracuda shiitake teriyaki

This is a very well-known fish that is normally cooked on the barbecue because of its lovely firm flesh. However, as I love teriyaki, I thought I would try cooking it this way, and this recipe is a definite winner.

SERVES: 4

Preparation time: 10 minutes plus
    40 minutes marinating time
Cooking time: 15 minutes

4 barracuda steaks (6oz each)
salt and freshly ground black pepper
6oz shiitake mushrooms, sliced
⅔ cup teriyaki sauce
8oz white radish, peeled
2 large carrots, peeled

method

1 Season the steaks, place in a dish in a single layer, and set aside for 20 minutes. Scatter over the sliced mushrooms, pour over the teriyaki sauce, and set aside to marinate for at least 20 minutes, or as long as possible.

2 Drain the barracuda, reserving the marinade and mushrooms, and cook on a preheated barbecue for 4 minutes each side.

3 Transfer the mushrooms and marinade to a pan and simmer gently for 4 minutes.

4 Slice the radish and carrots thinly and arrange in a heap on each plate. Top with the fish, pour over the mushroom sauce, and serve immediately.

Alternative fish:
mahi mahi, monkfish

Right: Barracuda shiitake teriyaki

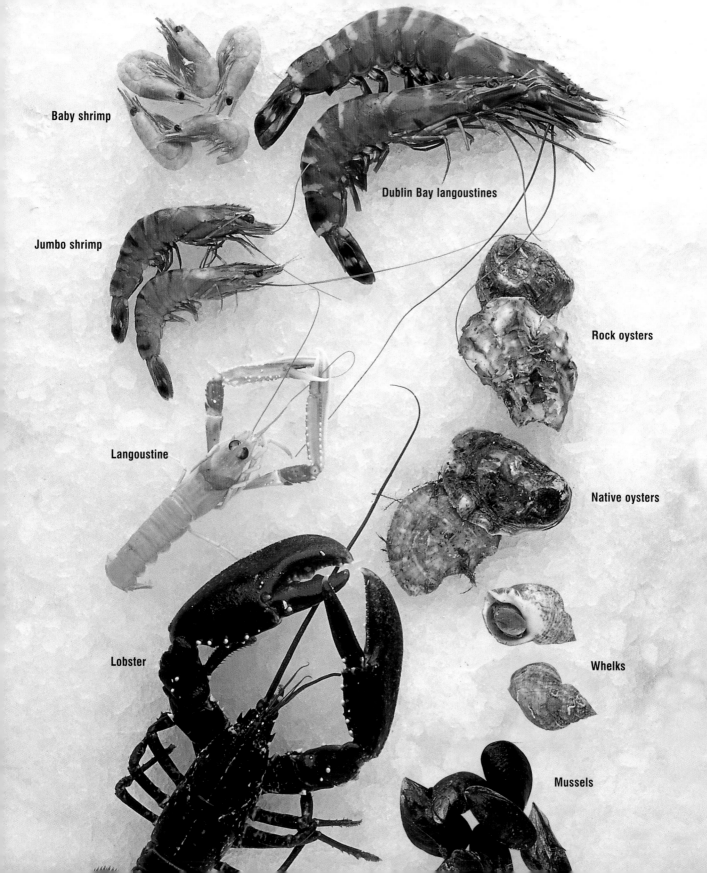

Baby shrimp

Dublin Bay langoustines

Jumbo shrimp

Rock oysters

Langoustine

Native oysters

Whelks

Lobster

Mussels

Spider crab

Scallops

Shellfish

Chowder clams

Crab

Littleneck clams

Razor clams

Shellfish

Aquatic invertebrates are believed to descend from creatures that lived on earth more than 200 million years ago and are divided into two main classes: crustaceans and molluscs. Most crustaceans are marine and include lobsters, crabs, and shrimp, but crayfish are found in fresh water. Crustaceans are very odd-looking creatures, but while they may not look like the most attractive of foods, it is well worth the effort involved in removing their delicious flesh. Crustaceans need to be very fresh and are best bought live, but you can also buy them ready cooked, as well, of course, as frozen or canned. Molluscs are divided into bivalves, such as clams, mussels, and oysters, which have a hinged shell, and gastropods, which have a single external shell and include abalone, conch, limpets, and whelks. There are two important things to remember when you are preparing molluscs: firstly, they should be soaked in water overnight in order to remove the sand (the exception to this is scallops, which can be simply cleaned), and shells that are open before cooking and those that are closed once cooked should be discarded or you could become ill.

Crustaceans

CRABS

Crabs have evolved so that they can walk or run sideways as well as burrow and swim. Their body is covered in a carapace and they also have a reduced abdomen, which is tucked under the body and is used as a pouch for eggs.

The segmented body has several pairs of legs, of which usually five pairs are for walking and two for sensing and smelling. They also have two pincers for fighting, feeding, and display. Crabs adapt to the changing environment and are thought to have advanced senses of smell and taste, which help them to mate and forage.

Crabs are quite adventurous and will travel hundreds of miles in a year for feeding and to breeding grounds. Most crabs are caught far from the shore in baited traps.

Like most crustaceans, crabs shed their shell and grow a new one. While the new shell is growing, it is soft and these so-called soft-shell crabs can be eaten whole (see below).

The sweetest meat is found in female crabs, but they are smaller in size than the males and their claws also tend to contain less flesh.

All crabs should be bought alive rather than cooked. The best way to cook crabs is to put them in cold salted water and bring them to a boil. This will ensure that the meat is tender; if you throw them into boiling water, their muscles contract and this can affect the flavor of the meat.

DUNGENESS CRAB *Cancer majister*
Found in Pacific waters from Alaska to southern California, the Dungeness crab inhabits eel-grass beds and muddy to sandy bottoms, from near the shore—most commonly—to waters more than 600 feet deep.

Dungeness crabs are brownish in color and have white-tipped claws. An average specimen measures around 8 inches and its large, powerful claws contain plenty of tasty flesh. They are very aggressive and care needs to be taken when handling them.

The male waits until the female is "molting" in order to mate and holds onto the female waiting for the molting to be complete. The female in excess of two million eggs, but only a few of these survive.

These crabs are scavengers but will also feed on molluscs, which they crush with their large claws.

SPIDER CRAB *Maja squinado*
The spider crab is spiny and pear shaped with long slender legs, thus resembling a large pink spider. Harmless to humans and not particularly aggressive, the spider crab's main defence is to camouflage itself: it has hairs on its shell that hold algae and debris in place, thus blending the crab into its environment.

Spider crabs live in deeper water in the winter, normally in depths up to 400 feet, but come closer to the shore in the summer months when temperatures rise. Like other crabs, the females carry the eggs, which take 60–75 days to mature before the larvae hatch. A female crab may hatch as many as 150,000 larvae.

The spider crabs found in the Atlantic measure about 8 inches across, but there is a giant species that originates around Japan that can grow up to 16 inches and has a claw span of 10 feet. This is not a crustacean for arachnophobes!

SOFT-SHELL CRAB
These are blue crabs (*Callinectes sapidus*) that have shed their shell in order to grow a new one. They tend to hide themselves under rocks and sand until the new shell grows, which is a quick process. Soft-shelled crabs are extremely delicate and do not keep or travel very well, so you will normally only find them in the summer months across the USA.

CRAYFISH various species including *Astacus fluviatilis*
Crayfish are also called crawfish or crawdad and are closely related to lobsters. Nearly all crayfish live in fresh water and most species are found in North America, particularly around Kentucky and Louisiana, although they are also found in Europe and throughout the world.

Crayfish usually measure about 2¾ inches long and have a joined head and mid-section, a segmented body, and eyes that are on moveable stalks. Their hard outer shell provides protection but does limit their growth. The smallest species of crayfish is about 1 inch long and is found in southeast USA; the largest, which is found near Tasmania, reaches up to 16 inches in length and can weigh 13lb.

Most crayfish live short lives—usually less than two years—so a high reproduction is important. The female crayfish can lay anything from 10 to 800 eggs, which will hatch in two to 20 weeks, depending on the temperature, and will stay attached until shortly after their second molt.

Crayfish have a wonderful flavor and, whatever their color when alive (sandy yellow, green, or dark brown), they turn a deep scarlet when cooked. Crayfish should ideally be bought live. There is a lot of wastage, so allow 8–12 per person. Keep the shells to make stock, soup, or sauce.

LANGOUSTINES *Nephrops Norvegicus*

Otherwise known as Norway lobsters; or Dublin Bay prawns, langoustines are usually around 8 inches long and are, in effect, small lobsters. They are pale orange/pink in color and the head and thorax have a non-segmented shell, while the long abdomen is segmented with a broad fan-like tail. Their eyes are large, black, and immovable. The colder the water in which langoustines live, the better the flavor of the meat.

Langoustines deteriorate rapidly on being caught so are usually cooked and frozen at sea. If you do find them live, they need to be cooked soon after buying; make sure they are still moving. Place the live langoustines in a pan of cold water and bring them slowly to a boil. Boil for 4 minutes then transfer them to a bowl of ice water to cool.

Unlike other crustaceans, langoustines do not change color when cooked, so be careful not to overcook them. Clean langoustines in the same way as shrimp, removing the black intestinal vein running down the back.

LOBSTERS

Lobsters are generally regarded as the finest crustaceans, as they have a firm, sweet flesh with a delicious flavor. They are also lower in saturated fat, cholesterol, and

calories than white chicken, which means that they are very good for you as well as tasty.

Each of the lobster's eyes is set on a moveable stalk and has up to 10,000 facets, which operate like many tiny eyes. These make it possible for the lobsters to detect motion in dim light on the ocean floor. They also have tiny hairs that cover the body, including the legs, and these are sensitive to touch.

If a lobster likes what it picks up, it will pass the object to its mouth, where more hairs detect taste. It also has two strong claws, one for crushing and one for tearing the flesh, and it uses these claws for gripping and shredding food. It normally walks forward on its eight legs, but if threatened, it will contract its tail forcefully and move backward quite rapidly.

Lobsters continue to grow throughout their lives, "molting" like crabs, but they grow very slowly, only reaching maturity at six years old. The lobsters normally served in restaurants weigh about 2lb 4oz each, which means they are about 10 years old. This explains the short supply of lobsters and their high cost. The largest lobster ever caught weighed more than 44lb and may have been 100 years old.

Lobsters must be alive when you cook them: a dead lobster is likely to give you extreme shellfish poisoning. Lobsters may be red, blue, albino, or dark with yellow spots when alive, but all lobsters turn red on cooking. The quickest and most humane way to kill a lobster is to push a knife into the back of its head through the brain: this will kill it instantly.

CANADIAN/AMERICAN LOBSTER *Homarus americanus*

These are found in large numbers around Canada and the North

American Atlantic. They closely resemble the Scottish/European lobster but are greener and the claws are slightly fleshier than those of their European cousins. They do make excellent eating, but do not have the same quality of meat as the Scottish. Canadian/American lobsters are airfreighted live to Europe to try to meet the increasing demand for lobsters and the decreasing supply of Scottish lobsters. Even taking into the account the cost of shipping, them, they are still cheaper to buy in Europe than Scottish/European ones.

SCOTTISH/EUROPEAN LOBSTER *Homarus gammarus*

These lobsters are considered to have the best flavor of all lobsters. They are a blue-black color and may be dotted with bright blue spots. Scottish/European lobsters are becoming increasingly difficult to find and therefore very expensive. However, because of their superior quality, they are definitely worth the price if you can find them.

SHRIMP

In the UK shrimp are known both as shrimp and as prawns; in fact in the fish trade the names indicate only size: shrimp less than 2 inches are known as shrimp. In the USA, all are called shrimp.

Shrimp are scavengers, eating plankton and anything they can find on the ocean floor. They have quite a thin exoskeleton and their color ranges from translucent brown, through greeny-gray to pink.

Shrimp are sold in different sizes, ranging from the tiny to the colossal. The sizes are marked by the number needed to weigh 1lb. The smallest are known as pop-corn shrimp and are about 100 to the pound. These are usually sold frozen or canned and used in sauces or for potted shrimp.

Small shrimp are 36–45 to the pound and medium shrimp are about 31–35 to the pound. Next in size are large shrimp at 21–30 to the pound, the extra-large at 16–20 to the pound, and finally the jumbo shrimp at 10–15 to the pound.

Depending on where you live, almost all the shrimp you can buy will have been frozen by the time they reach the market or fish store. Some will be sold frozen while others are defrosted and sold as "fresh" shrimp. Make sure that these "fresh" shrimp are kept on ice and have no ammonia smell.

The large sizes and above are sometimes sold with their heads on and un-peeled; these are often known as "green shrimp." These can be cooked intact using the shells to keep in flavors and juices; they are great cooked on the barbecue, poached, or broiled. Smaller shrimp are usually sold ready-peeled.

Molluscs

CLAMS numerous varieties

Clams feed upon plankton through a siphon, which acts like a snorkel. Within this are millions of little hairs that keep water circulating. Despite looking sturdy, clam shells are quite fragile and should be handled with care. All clams have a sweet flavor and a firm texture; most can either be cooked or eaten raw. Discard any with a broken shell or that is open before cooking as it may be dead and this will cause food poisoning. You should also discard any clam that remains closed once cooked.

LITTLENECK CLAM *Protothaca staminea*

This is the most commonly available clam and the one that most people are familiar with. Littlenecks are fairly small—1½–2¾ inches—with smooth creamy shells. They can be very gritty so it is best to leave them in salted water overnight, changing the water a couple of times, to remove any sand or grit. Littlenecks are very tender and are best eaten steamed or in sauces.

RAZOR CLAM *Ensis ensis*
These very strange-looking clams resemble an old-fashioned razor, with a long tube-like shell that is brown with some gold striping. The flesh tends to ooze out of the ends of the shells in a wormlike fashion. To ensure the clams are fresh, tap the shells and they should retract back into their shells. Often the look of these clams will put people off; if you are nervous, remove the flesh from the shell and chop it into pieces before eating it. Razor clams are worth trying for their delicious flavor.

CHOWDER CLAM *Mercenaria mercenaria*
These are often called large clams in the fish markets. They are very fleshy and do not lend themselves to being eaten raw as the meat can be quite tough. These clams also take longer to cook than their smaller cousins, but they do have a good flavor as well as a slightly meatier texture.

MUSSELS
Mussels attach themselves to rocks and each other using their beards (byssus) and can live in large congregations. Mussels feed on particles in the water, which is drawn in through a gap in the shell and expelled through an outflow tube.

BLACK-SHELL/COMMON MUSSELS
These coldwater mussels have a smooth bluish black shell, which looks pear shaped, and can grow up to 4 inches long, although they are generally found at only half this size.

Black-shell/common mussels are the most succulent of all mussels with a fairly sweet flavor. The female's flesh is a lovely orange color, while the male has a lighter, cream-colored flesh. Although some people maintain that the flesh of the female is better than that of the male, I do not think that there is much difference between the two.

OYSTERS
Oysters tend to evoke a strong response in most people—you either love them or hate them. I have to confess that they are not one of my favorite shellfish. They do, however, have a reputation as an aphrodisiac, which has helped increase their popularity. Unfortunately, it has also helped to decrease the stocks available. Because of centuries of over fishing and disease, most oysters are now cultivated and oyster cultivation has become highly profitable, even though it is a labor-intensive and very slow business. Rock oysters are grown for three years before being moved and "fattened" for a year. As their name implies, native oysters grow wild and can take up to seven years to mature, hence their higher price.

Oysters feed by filtering food particles from the surrounding water: the quantity of water pumped by a large, healthy oyster may approach 4 gallons an hour. Any matter brought into the oysters with the water is collected by mucus on the gills and large amounts of silt are discharged in this manner. (A pearl is the result of a tiny irritant, like a grain of sand, becoming imbedded in the oyster.)

Oysters are said to be in season when there is an "r" in the month, but this applies only to wild oysters, which are protected from May to

August, which is their breeding season. You can eat farmed oysters all year round.

NATIVE OYSTER
The Pacific, Eastern, and Olympia oysters are sold across the USA and the names indicate where they are harvested. Along the Atlantic seaboard they include local varieties such as Bluepoint, Cape Cod, and Indian River.

ROCK OYSTER genus *Crassostrea*
Rock oysters are longer and rougher looking than native ones, are often dark gray in color and have rather coarse flesh. Although they are still good eaten raw in the traditional way, they lend themselves more to being cooked.

SCALLOPS family Pectinidae
Scallops are delicious molluscs— true treasures from the deep— though they are expensive. Venus is said to have emerged from the sea on a scallop shell and, no doubt as a result, scallops are believed by some to be an aphrodisiac.

Scallops are probably best known for their beautiful and distinctive scalloped shell, which is normally a salmon pink/orange color. The edible part of the scallop is the white muscle that opens and closes the two shells; this has a soft fleshy texture and a delicate flavor. The roe, which is known as the "coral," is also edible and is a bright orange in color.

Unlike other bivalves (such as mussels and clams), scallops do not burrow in the sand or rocks, but rather swim above the sea bed by opening and closing their shells.

Scallops are primarily harvested by dredging, but this can cause them to become quite gritty. The best scallops are Diver scallops, which,

as the name implies, are caught by people diving and collecting them.

Always take care not to overcook scallops as they become tough; as soon as they become white/opaque they are ready. Try to buy fresh scallops in the shell, otherwise buy the tubs of scallops "dry" not "wet." The wet ones absorb too much water and do not have much flavor.

SEA AND BAY SCALLOPS
Although they differ in size—the sea (*Pecten maximus*) is larger than the bay (*Pecten opercularis*)—there is very little difference in flavor between them. Bay scallops are normally sold out of the shell and you need to allocate at least 10–12 per person as they are literally a mouthful. Because of their larger size, sea scallops lend themselves better to ceviche, pan-frying, and baking.

WHELKS family Buccinidae
These marine snails have a whitish conical shell and are found on mud flats. They are particularly common on the coasts of the Atlantic and English Channel.

Whelks are best cooked for about 8–10 minutes in salted water—any longer and they become tough—and eaten with bread and butter or with mayonnaise or vinegar.

Thai shrimp curry

Thai food happens to be one of my favorite foods—after Italian that is! And this recipe is one of my favorite Thai dishes—there's nothing better than eating this with your partner or family for a relaxing night at home. Enjoy!

SERVES: 4

Preparation time: 10 minutes
Cooking time: 45 minutes

1 tsp olive oil
1 garlic clove, finely chopped
5 shallots, finely chopped
2 Tbsp Thai green curry paste
3 Tbsp good fish stock
14fl oz can coconut milk
20 raw jumbo shrimp, peeled and
    deveined
2 Tbsp chopped cilantro
coconut rice to serve (optional)

method

1 Heat the olive oil in a pan and sauté the garlic and shallots over a medium heat for 2 minutes. Stir in the Thai green curry paste and cook for a further 2 minutes, stirring continuously.

2 Add the fish stock and cook for 15 minutes over a medium heat, then stir in the coconut milk and cook for a further 15 minutes.

3 Add the shrimp and cook for 10 minutes until the shrimp are pink in color. Stir in the chopped cilantro and serve immediately, with coconut rice if desired.

1 Raw shrimp are often peeled before cooking, but if you can, leave the shells on as they will add flavor to the shrimp.

2 Insert a sharp knife just behind the head. Cut down the back all the way to the tail, so that the shrimp is only attached at the head.

3 Using your fingers or a knife, pull out the black intestinal vein on one side. Repeat on the other side and then wash thoroughly.

4 These shrimp are now butterflied and are ready for barbecuing, broiling, or pan-frying.

Shrimp soufflé

This has to be one of the best recipes in the book! Don't be scared of making a soufflé—they are actually relatively easy. The main thing you need to ensure is that the ingredients are cold before you combine them.

SERVES: 4

Preparation time: 40 minutes
Cooking time: 35 minutes

1 Tbsp extra virgin olive oil
4 oz jumbo shrimp, peeled and cleaned
½ garlic clove, finely chopped
½ small red chili, seeded and finely chopped
½ tsp finely chopped Italian flat-leaf parsley
dash vodka
salt and freshly ground black pepper
1 egg yolk
¼ cup heavy cream
2 egg whites, chilled
juice of ¼ lemon
butter to grease ramekins

Alternative shellfish:
lobster, crab

method

1 Heat the oil in a skillet and add the shrimp. Stir until they change color, then add the chopped garlic, chili, and parsley. Deglaze the pan with the vodka and continue cooking for a further 3–4 minutes.

2 Remove the shrimp from the pan and leave to cool to room temperature. (Make sure that they are completely cool before continuing; if they are too hot, the egg will begin to cook.) Place the cooled shrimp in a food processor and blitz with a teaspoon of salt and the egg yolk until smooth. Refrigerate for 30 minutes.

3 Remove the mix from the refrigerator and transfer it into a stainless-steel bowl. Place the bowl into another bowl full of ice, then add the cream a little at a time, incorporating it at first by drizzling it from a spoon in small circles. Stir in a pinch of pepper and refrigerate again.

4 Preheat the oven to 325°F.

5 In another large bowl, whisk the egg whites with a pinch of salt until they form stiff peaks, then carefully stir in the lemon juice.

6 Remove the shrimp mixture from the refrigerator and, using a wooden spoon, mix it into the egg white using a fast circular motion until smooth.

7 Rub the insides of 4 individual ramekins with butter. Half fill them with the mixture. Place a sheet of parchment paper in a roasting pan to stop the ramekins from moving, then place the ramekins in the roasting pan, leaving plenty of space between each one. Fill the tray with hot water to a depth of ½ inch and place in the oven. Cook the soufflés for 30 minutes until risen and golden brown. Serve immediately.

Jumbo shrimp Portuguese style

When I'm in Portugal, I go out of my way to visit my favorite restaurant there. The food is amazing and the menu is full of mouthwatering fish dishes, which inspired me to come up with this one.

SERVES: 4

Preparation time: 10 minutes
Cooking time: 8 minutes

2 Tbsp olive oil
2 Tbsp unsalted butter
8 raw jumbo shrimp, cleaned and butterflied
6 garlic cloves, finely chopped
3 dry chilies, crushed
1 bunch green onions, trimmed and finely chopped
3 Tbsp dry white wine
2 lemons
garlic bread to serve

method

1 Heat the oil and butter in a large skillet, add the butterflied shrimp and cook for 3–4 minutes until they become a nice pink color.

2 Add the garlic, chilli, and green onions and cook for 3 minutes, then add the white wine and the juice of 1 lemon, and continue cooking until half the liquid has evaporated.

3 Cut the other lemon into wedges. Serve the shrimp with garlic bread and lemon wedges.

Alternative shellfish:
scallops, langoustines

Shrimp with brandy pâté

Pâté is normally associated with liver, but as I have a fish restaurant I tried making it with shrimp and really liked the result. This is a great recipe for a summer picnic—it's light and refreshing and it travels well.

SERVES: 4

Preparation time: 15 minutes plus
    2 hours marinating time

1lb 2oz cooked and peeled shrimp
2 Tbsp brandy
3 garlic cloves, peeled and finely
    chopped
pinch of paprika
1 tsp each salt and freshly ground
    black pepper
1 egg yolk
1lb 12oz butter, melted
3 Tbsp heavy cream
3 jumbo shrimp, cooked and peeled
3 lemon slices

method

1 Marinate the shrimp in the brandy, garlic, and paprika for about 2 hours in the refrigerator.

2 Drain the shrimp, reserving the marinade, then blend in a food processor until smooth. Add salt and pepper, egg yolk, and melted butter and process until butter is completely amalgamated.

3 Put the processor on a low speed and add 3 tablespoons of the marinade liquid and the cream. Blend until both have been absorbed into the mixture.

4 Line a terrine dish with plastic wrap and pour the mixture into it. Level the top with a spatula and decorate with lemon slices and jumbo shrimp. Refrigerate for at least 30 minutes, then remove from the terrine dish by pulling the plastic wrap.

Alternative shellfish:
white crab meat

Potted shrimp

This is quite an old-fashioned recipe but I really love it! There is a lot of butter in this recipe, but don't let this put you off—when you come to eat it, you can lift off the butter and eat only the shrimp.

SERVES: 4

Preparation time: 15 minutes
Cooking time: 10 minutes

½lb fresh baby shrimp
1 tsp olive oil
¾lb unsalted butter
1 bay leaf
½ tsp ground mace
salt and freshly ground black pepper
pinch of cayenne pepper
thin slices of brown toast to serve

method

1 Pan-fry the shrimp in olive oil for about 3 minutes until cooked. Remove shrimp from the pan and set aside to cool, then peel them.

2 Melt 1 cup of butter in the pan and stir in the shrimp, bay leaf, and ground mace and season with salt, black pepper, and cayenne pepper. Cook over a low heat for 4 minutes. Discard the bay leaf and distribute the shrimp between 4 ramekins.

3 Clarify the remaining butter: cook it over a low heat until it is melted and foaming, then strain through cheesecloth. Completely cover the shrimp with the butter.

4 Leave to cool before refrigerating. Serve with thin slices of brown toast.

Right: Shrimp with brandy pâté

1 Holding the body of the langoustine with one hand, pull off the head with your other hand.

2 Holding the langoustine between your thumbs and forefingers, press down on the shell until it makes a cracking sound.

3 Turn the langoustine upside down and pull the shell away from the meat.

4 Pull the shell toward the tail and extract the meat. Remove the black intestinal vein running down the back.

Langoustine bisque

This is a more time-consuming recipe than most of the others in this book, but it is well worth the effort if you can make the time. Don't use frozen shellfish for this recipe as they will not give you the rich flavor you require.

SERVES: 4

Preparation time: 30 minutes
Cooking time: 1 hour

5½lb live langoustines
4 Tbsp olive oil
1 head of garlic, separated into
  cloves and peeled
1 head celery, peeled and diced
3 carrots, peeled and diced
1 onion, peeled and chopped
1 leek, peeled and chopped
2 Tbsp brandy
2½ quarts fish stock
2 Tbsp tomato paste
10 black peppercorns
1 Tbsp sea salt
1 bunch fresh parsley

method

1 Put the live langoustines in cold water and bring them slowly to a boil. Boil for 4 minutes, then transfer them to a bowl of ice water to cool.

2 Prepare the langoustines following the steps above. Reserve the shells and chop the meat.

3 In a large skillet, heat the oil and garlic until smoking. Add the langoustine shells and cook for 4–5 minutes, then add the celery, carrots, onion, and leek and cook for 2 minutes. Deglaze the pan with the brandy and fish stock, then stir in the tomato paste, peppercorns, and sea salt.

4 Bring back to a boil and skim off any fat, then simmer, uncovered, for 40–45 minutes, skimming again if necessary. Add most of the parsley leaves, reserving some for garnish, and continue simmering until the liquid has reduced by half.

5 Pass the bisque through a strainer then strain through 2 layers of damp cheesecloth. Return the liquid to a gentle boil then stir in the langoustine meat.

6 Serve the bisque in large bowls with parsley leaves scattered on top and a drizzle of extra virgin olive oil.

Alternative shellfish:
lobster, shrimp

Broiled langoustines

I love langoustines: they are really delicate with a sweet, distinct flavor. This is a fantastic way to cook them—a really simple recipe but full of flavor.

Alternative shellfish:
shrimp, scallops

SERVES: 4

Preparation time: 10 minutes plus
　1 hour marinating time
Cooking time: 5 minutes

16 prepared langoustines
1 fresh chili, seeded and chopped
2 garlic cloves, crushed
juice of 1 lemon
1 tsp crushed sea salt
1 Tbsp extra virgin olive oil
tartar sauce or sweet chili sauce
　and salad to serve

method

1 Marinate the prepared langoustines in the chili, garlic, lemon juice, salt, and oil.

2 Place under a hot broiler and cook for 5 minutes.

3 Serve with tartar sauce or sweet chili sauce and salad.

Seafood risotto

Risotto and fish is a great combination! You can choose whatever fish you like for this dish; just make sure you use a good fish stock. Add stock to the risotto gradually: if you add too much you will end up with soup instead.

SERVES: 4

Preparation time: 30 minutes
Cooking time: 30 minutes

1½ quarts fish stock
6 Tbsp butter
1 medium onion, finely chopped
2 garlic cloves, finely chopped
1 bay leaf, torn in half
1¾ cups risotto rice
⅛lb mussels, scrubbed, beards and
    barnacles removed
⅔ cup white wine such as Prosecco
6oz firm fish fillet (e.g. cod,
    salmon, haddock), skinned and
    cut into 2-inch pieces
2 Tbsp chopped fresh parsley
1 Tbsp chopped chives
salt and freshly ground
    black pepper

method

1 Pour the stock into a large pan and bring to a gentle simmer.

2 Meanwhile, melt 2 tablespoons of butter in a large pan, add the onion, garlic, and 2 bay leaf halves, and sauté for 5–8 minutes until soft. Stir in the rice. Cook, stirring, for about 30 seconds.

3 Gradually add the stock, a ladleful at a time, to the rice, stirring and adding more stock as each batch is absorbed. The total cooking time will be about 20 minutes, at the end of which the rice should be *al dente*. Season well to taste. Set aside.

4 Meanwhile, place the mussels in a separate pan, add the wine, cover tightly, and cook over a high heat for 3–5 minutes, shaking the pan frequently, until the shells have opened. Strain the pan juices through a fine sieve and reserve. Discard any mussels that have remained closed.

5 Return the risotto to a low heat and stir in the remaining butter. Add some of the reserved pan juices if the risotto is a little dry. Stir in the fish, mussels, parsley, and chives and season to taste. Cook for a further 1–2 minutes until the fish is tender and just flakes. Discard the bay leaf halves.

6 Spoon the risotto into 4 large warmed bowls, sprinkle with black pepper, and serve immediately.

Crayfish salad with mango and citrus dressing

If you like crayfish, you will enjoy this great summer salad. When mixing leaves and dressing together, put the dressing in a stainless-steel bowl, then add the rest of the ingredients and toss gently to ensure an even coating.

SERVES: 4

Preparation time: 15 minutes

1 egg yolk
1 tsp English mustard
6 Tbsp olive oil
juice of 1 orange
juice of 1 lemon
juice of 1 lime
5 cups baby spinach leaves
½ cup toasted croutons
14oz crayfish meat
2 mangoes, peeled and diced
1 pinch of paprika
salt and freshly ground black pepper

Alternative shellfish:
crab, shrimp

method

1 In a large stainless steel bowl, whisk the egg yolk and mustard together. Add the oil a little at a time, whisking continuously, until you have a mayonnaise-like consistency. Gently whisk in the orange, lemon, and lime juices.

2 In another bowl, mix together the baby spinach, croutons, and half the dressing until the leaves and croutons are evenly coated.

3 Mix the crayfish with the remaining dressing, half the mango, and the paprika and make sure it is well coated. Season to taste.

4 Place the spinach leaves in a pile on each plate, top with the crayfish mix, and scatter over remaining mango before serving.

PREPARING LOBSTER

1 Place the lobster on a board and pierce the center of the head with a sharp knife to kill it.

2 Pull the knife toward the tail in a smooth action. Cut through the tail.

3 Cut through the head so that you end up with 2 lobster halves.

4 Using the back of a knife, smash the claws a couple of times. This will make it easier for you to remove the meat from them.

Lobster thermidor

There are lots of variations of this dish but this is the way I cook it and my customers seem to love it! Make sure that you use live lobsters as this will provide the best result. I introduced my daughter, Laura, to shellfish with this dish.

SERVES: 4

Preparation time: 20 minutes
Cooking time: 5 minutes

2 live lobsters (14oz–1lb 2oz each), boiled for 5 minutes only
¾ cup butter
16 green onions, finely chopped
2 Tbsp all-purpose flour
2 tsp English mustard
¼ cup white wine
1 cup milk
¼ cup heavy cream
2 Tbsp finely chopped parsley
salt and freshly ground black pepper
4oz cheese (Parmesan, Dolcelatte, Stilton, or Gruyère)

method

1 Using a sharp knife, cut the lobster in half lengthwise. Lift the meat from the tail and the body. Crack the claws and prise the meat from them. Remove the intestinal vein and discard. Cut the meat into bite-size pieces, cover, and refrigerate. Wash the lobster shell, drain, and dry.

2 Heat ¼ cup of the butter in a skillet and cook the green onions for 2 mintues. Add the flour and the mustard and cook for a further 1 minute. Remove from the heat and gradually add the wine and the milk. Return to the heat and cook, stirring continuously to avoid any lumps, until the mixture has thickened.

3 Stir in the cream, parsley, and lobster meat and season; heat gently. Spoon this mixture into the lobster shells, sprinkle with cheese, and dot with the remaining butter.

4 Place under a preheated broiler and cook for 2 minutes, or until the top is lightly browned.

Alternative shellfish:
jumbo shrimp

Lobster in Grand Marnier and kumquat sauce

Cooking lobster this way really brings out its flavor. Again, please be sure to find live lobsters as this will make all the difference to the taste. If you can't find kumquats, clementines or oranges will work just as well.

SERVES: 4

Preparation time: 10 minutes
Cooking time: 15 minutes

4 live lobsters (14oz–1lb 2oz each)
salt and freshly ground black pepper
2 Tbsp extra virgin olive oil
¼ cup unsalted butter
4 shallots, finely chopped
4 garlic cloves, finely chopped
2 tsp chopped cilantro
2 tsp brown sugar
12 kumquats, peeled
3 Tbsp Grand Marnier

method

1 Cook the live lobsters for 5 minutes until pink. Open the lobster by cutting in half lengthwise and remove the green intestinal vein. Preheat the oven to 375°F.

2 Season the lobster with salt and pepper and 2 tablespoons of olive oil and place under the broiler, shell side up, for 5 minutes until the meat is lightly browned.

3 In a large skillet heat the butter, shallots, garlic, cilantro, sugar, and kumquats. Cook the fruit until it is glistening and the sugar has caramelized the fruit, then add the Grand Marnier and 1 cup of water.

4 Pour the sauce and fruit over the lobster and cook in the oven for 10 minutes. Place a lobster half on each of 4 individual plates and pour over the sauce.

Alterative fish:
jumbo shrimp

Lobster burgers with chili relish

Burgers or fish cakes are normally made with inexpensive fish or shellfish but if you really fancy a treat then this is the one for you. You can, of course, serve the burger in a roll—an alternative version of fast food!

SERVES: 4

Preparation time: 10 minutes
Cooking time: 9 minutes

1lb 2oz fresh lobster meat
3 Tbsp rice flour or cornstarch
1 small red chili, seeded and finely
    chopped
2 garlic cloves, finely chopped
2 green onions, finely chopped
2 tsp finely chopped Italian flat-leaf
    parsley
2 egg yolks
1 tsp soy sauce
salt and freshly ground black pepper
4 salad leaves
chili relish
chunky fries to serve

method

1 Preheat the oven to 350°F.

2 In a large bowl, place the lobster meat, flour, chili, garlic, green onions, parsley, egg yolks, and soy sauce, season with salt and pepper, and stir together with your hands until the mixture is smooth and your fingers are dry.

3 Divide the mixture into 4 equal portions, roll into balls, and flatten slightly with the palm of your hand to form burgers.

4 Heat the broiler and sear the burgers on each side. Transfer to a baking sheet and finish in the oven for about 6 minutes. Serve on top of the salad leaves, with chili relish and chunky fries.

Right: Lobster burgers with chili relish

PREPARING CRAB

1 Lay the crab upside down on a chopping board.

2 Insert a sharp knife between the mouth plates and the eyes of the crab.

3 Using the knife as a lever, remove the top shell, which will remove the inside of the crab.

4 You will end up with a shell that resembles that of a scallop. Pull off the claws.

5 This is how the crab should look once you have taken it all apart.

6 Using the back of the knife, smash the claws to get at the meat. (You may want to cover the claws with a cloth as this can be messy.)

7 Once you have cracked the claw, the meat will come out in one piece with only a thin "plastic" piece in the middle of the meat.

8 Using a spoon, remove the brown meat from the shell, making sure that you scoop out all the solid brown meat from the sides.

Creole crab

This is a very good recipe for crab, with lots of flavor. For an alternative dish, place the crab in ramekins, sprinkle with ⅔ cup each of breadcrumbs and butter and cook in the oven at 350˚F for 10 minutes.

SERVES: 6

Preparation time: 15 minutes

14oz white crab meat
3 eggs, hard boiled and shelled
1 tsp wholegrain mustard
3 Tbsp extra virgin olive oil
pinch of cayenne pepper
pinch of paprika
2 Tbsp sherry
2 Tbsp chopped parsley
½ cup light cream
3 green onions, finely sliced
salt and freshly ground black pepper
6 tomatoes, sliced, to serve
6 sprigs basil to garnish

method

1 Make sure your crab meat has been well picked and there is no shell or cartilage in the meat. Flake the meat into a bowl, if possible keeping the pieces fairly large.

2 Remove the egg yolks from the hard-boiled eggs, place in a bowl, and crumble them with a fork. Add the mustard, oil, cayenne pepper, and paprika and mash until you form a paste, then stir in the sherry and the parsley.

3 Chop the egg whites and add them to the yolk mixture with the cream and green onions. Mix well and then gently fold in the crab meat. Season to taste and serve immediately with sliced tomatoes and garnished with basil.

Crab claws pan-fried with pesto

As crabs tend to lose their claws, most fish stores will have some to buy, so you don't need to get the whole crab. You can adjust this recipe and make the claws with garlic, chili, and olive oil if you prefer. Either way, this is a wonderful meal. The pesto can be kept for up to a week as long as it is covered with olive oil.

SERVES: 4

Preparation time: 10 minutes
Cooking time: 6 minutes

4 Tbsp extra virgin olive oil
12 large crab claws, cracked but
   still in the shell
8 garlic cloves
2 tsp chopped Italian
   flat-leaf parsley
⅓ cup dry white wine
toasted ciabatta to serve

Pesto
1½ cups freshly grated Pecorino
½ cup freshly grated Parmesan
1 cup fresh basil leaves
1 Tbsp sun-dried tomatoes
2 Tbsp toasted pine nuts
2 garlic cloves, finely chopped
1 cup extra virgin olive oil
salt and freshly ground black pepper

method

1 First make the pesto: blitz all the ingredients together in a food processor. If you are not using it straight away, ensure that the pesto is covered with olive oil.

2 Heat the oil in a large skillet, then add the crab claws, garlic, and the parsley. Cook for 2 minutes until the garlic is a golden color, stirring occasionally.

3 Add the wine and pesto to the pan and cook for 4 minutes. Serve hot with thin slices of toasted ciabatta.

Crab and vegetable frittata

Fritatta is the Italian version of the omelette and is probably the most versatile dish to make with eggs. I find it marries very well with shellfish as well as with vegetables and cheese. I remember tasting this particular one in Soho, New York, and I thought I'd share it with you.

SERVES: 4

Preparation time: 10 minutes
Cooking time: 25 minutes

8 eggs
1 Tbsp heavy cream
salt and ground black pepper
1 red onion, finely chopped
2 zucchini, diced
1 red bell pepper, diced
1 yellow bell pepper, diced
1 Tbsp olive oil
3½oz white crab meat
1 Tbsp chopped parsley
mixed leaf salad to serve

method

1 Whisk the eggs together with the cream and season. Preheat the oven to 375°F.

2 Pan-fry the onion, zucchini, and bell peppers for 3 minutes in olive oil, then add the crab meat and continue cooking for a further 3 minutes.

3 Line an ovenproof dish with parchment paper and lay the vegetable and crab mixture along the bottom of the dish. Pour over the egg mixture and cook in the oven for 10–15 minutes until the egg has risen and is golden brown. Remove and set aside to cool completely. Sprinkle with chopped parsley.

4 Serve the frittata, cut into wedges, with a mixed leaf salad.

Alternative fish:
lobster, scallop, or shrimp meat

Spider crab with linguine and zucchini

While spider crabs are not the most attractive looking of shellfish, their meat is a lot sweeter than that of Dungeness crab and it makes this sauce very tasty. You can, of course, use other crabs for this recipe if you prefer.

SERVES: 4

Preparation time: 30 minutes plus
  20 minutes cooling time
Cooking time: 50 minutes

4 medium live spider crabs
  (1lb each)
⅔ cup extra virgin olive oil
1 bunch of green onions, finely
  chopped
6 garlic cloves, finely chopped
2 red chilies, finely chopped
1lb 2oz linguine
3 zucchini, diced
2 Tbsp finely chopped Italian
  flat-leaf parsley
¼ cup white wine
juice of 1 lemon

Alternative fish:
Dungeness crab

method

1 Preheat the oven to 350°F. Place the crabs in a large pot of cold water and bring slowly to a boil. Cook for 20 minutes, then cool in a large bowl of ice water for about 20 minutes.

2 Remove the meat from the crabs, reserving the crab shells. Crack the claws, place them in a roasting pan with ½ cup of olive oil, half the green onions, half the garlic, and 1 chili, and roast in the oven for 16 minutes.

3 Meanwhile, cook the pasta according to the packet instructions, draining it 1 minute before the end of the recommended cooking time.

4 In a skillet, heat the remaining extra virgin olive oil, garlic, chili, and green onions and the zucchini. Stir, cook for 2 minutes, then add the crab meat and 1 tablespoon of parsley. Deglaze the pan with the white wine and add the linguine. Sauté the pasta and crab for 1 minute, add lemon juice, and stir.

5 Using tongs, remove the pasta and crab meat from the pan and divide between the crab shells. Remove the claws from the oven and set alongside the body. Sprinkle with remaining parsley and serve immediately.

1 Make sure none of the mussels is open, as this means they are either dead or full of sand. Discard any open mussels.

2 Using a knife remove the "beard" from all the mussels; you will need to pull some of this out.

3 Place the mussels in a bowl of clean salted water and leave overnight to remove any sand or grit. Change the water at least twice.

Adriatic fish stew

Stew is not really quite the word to describe this dish, but soup doesn't work either. Whatever you decide to call it, however, this is a favorite recipe of mine and a dish that I eat every time I am in Italy.

SERVES: 6

Preparation time: 20 minutes
Cooking time: 50 minutes

14oz whole small fish (e.g. mackerel, red mullet, sea bream)
1lb 2oz fish fillets (e.g. sole, sea bass, cod, gray or red mullet)
10oz small squid
14oz fresh mussels in shells
10oz raw shrimp
1 onion, peeled and cut into quarters
1 carrot, peeled and cut into quarters
2 stalks celery, peeled and chopped
6 garlic cloves
2½ cups dry white wine
14oz ripe plum tomatoes
⅓ cup extra virgin olive oil
2 red chilies, seeded and chopped
pinch of saffron strands
salt and freshly ground black pepper
½ cup chopped Italian flat-leaf parsley

method

1 Gut and scale the whole fish, if your fish store hasn't already done so. Wash thoroughly in running water and cut off the heads. Cut the fillets into 1-inch pieces.

2 Trim and rinse the squid and cut into ½-inch-wide rings. Wash and scrape the mussels and discard any that are open. Wash and shell the shrimp, removing any dark vein-like intestines.

3 Place the onion, carrot, celery, mushrooms, 3 whole garlic cloves (peeled), and whole small fish in a pan and cover with 1 quart of cold, slightly salted water. Bring to a boil, then immediately reduce the heat and simmer for 20 minutes.

4 Meanwhile heat a heavy-based pan, place the cleaned mussels inside, cover, and cook for 2–3 minutes until they begin to open. Add ½ cup of white wine and cook until all the mussels are cooked and open. (Discard any that remain closed.) Strain the mussel stock and remove the mussels from their shells (leaving 8 in the shell for garnish). Add the mussel stock to the fish stock and keep mussels to one side.

5 Peel and chop the tomatoes and the remaining 3 garlic cloves. Pour the extra virgin olive oil into a large pan, add the chopped garlic, tomatoes, cleaned squid, shelled shrimp, and chopped chilies. Stir in 2 cups of white wine, cover the pan, and simmer for 15 minutes. Add the saffron strands and salt and pepper to taste.

6 Remove the whole fish from the stock and separate the fish from the bones. Discard the bones and add the fish to the tomato sauce.

7 Add the fish fillets, stock, and mussels to the tomato sauce and correct the seasoning. Serve garnished with chopped parsley and the reserved mussels in the shell.

Mussels diablo

This is a spicy dish but is great for the day after a few drinks. Adjust the amount of chili to suit your own taste and serve lots of lovely crusty bread to dip into the sauce.

SERVES: 4

Preparation time: 10 minutes
Cooking time: 20–25 minutes

3½lb mussels, cleaned
2 Tbsp olive oil
3 garlic cloves, finely chopped
6 red chilies, seeded and finely
    chopped
2 Tbsp Italian flat-leaf parsley,
    finely chopped
1 cup dry white wine
14oz canned chopped tomatoes
toasted ciabatta to serve

method

1 Discard any mussels that are open. Heat half the oil in a large pan and add the mussels, garlic, chili, and half the parsley. Cover and simmer over medium heat for 4–5 minutes.

2 After 4 minutes, begin to remove mussels that have opened; after 6 minutes, remove and discard any that have not opened.

3 Clean the pan, heat the remaining oil, and add mussels, wine, and chopped tomatoes. Cook for 15 minutes. Stir in the remainder of the parsley.

4 Serve the mussels hot in bowls with toasted sliced ciabatta.

Mussels with herb breadcrumbs, au gratin

I love mussels in lots of different ways but I find this to be very tasty and it also works very well with clams. If you wish, you can add pesto to the breadcrumbs, which will give a lovely flavor to the mussels.

SERVES: 4

Preparation time: 10 minutes
Cooking time: 6 minutes

3½ cups white breadcrumbs
2 Tbsp fresh basil leaves
2 Tbsp Italian flat-leaf parsley
2 Tbsp finely chopped lemon thyme
2 garlic cloves
2 marinated anchovies
salt and freshly ground black pepper
3 Tbsp unsalted butter
¼ cup extra virgin olive oil
20 large mussels, open
   in the ½ shell
lemon wedges and
   salad to serve

method

1 Preheat the broiler. In a food processor, blend the breadcrumbs, basil, parsley, lemon thyme, garlic, anchovies, salt, and pepper until the crumbs are light green in color, then add the butter and the olive oil.

2 Fill each mussel with some of the breadcrumb mixture and place the mussels on a baking sheet. Cook under the preheated broiler for about 5–6 minutes until brown and crispy. Serve hot with lemon wedges and salad.

Alternative shellfish:
clams

Razor clams with Asian herbs and noodles

Razor clams are not very well known, but I have to say I love them. This Asian-inspired recipe brings out their great flavor and looks impressive on the plate.

SERVES: 4

Preparation time: 10 minutes
Cooking time: 18 minutes

¼ cup sesame oil
2 red chilies, chopped
4 garlic cloves, finely sliced
1 tsp chopped fresh gingerroot
12 large razor clams, washed
3 cups bean sprouts
¾ cup sliced green beans
1lb egg noodles, cooked in boiling
   water until tender
2 Tbsp soy sauce
1 Tbsp oyster sauce
salt and freshly ground black pepper
1 bunch green onions, finely
   chopped
2 Tbsp chopped cilantro

method

1 Preheat the oven to 275°F. Heat 2 tablespoons of the sesame oil in a wok and stir-fry half the chilies, half the garlic, and half the ginger for 1–2 minutes. Add the clams, cover, and cook until the clams have opened. Discard any clams that remain unopened.

2 Remove the clams from the wok, place in a roasting pan, and bake in the oven for 10 minutes.

3 Meanwhile, in the same wok, heat the remaining oil and add remaining garlic, chili, and ginger along with the bean sprouts and green beans. Stir-fry for 2 minutes, then stir in the noodles, soy sauce, and oyster sauce and continue cooking for a further 4 minutes. Season to taste.

4 Using tongs, place the noodles on each of 4 plates, arrange 3 clams on top of each pile of noodles, and pour over any remaining juices. Scatter over the chopped green onions and cilantro and serve immediately.

Alternative shellfish:
littleneck clams

Clams in their own juice

This is the best way of cooking clams, when they're fresh and full of flavor. A lot of people add wine to this dish, but I think that it spoils the taste of the clams; with water they retain the freshness of the sea.

SERVES: 4

Preparation time: 10 minutes
Cooking time: 10 minutes

½ cup extra virgin olive oil
3 shallots, finely chopped
2 garlic cloves, crushed
½ chili, seeded and finely chopped
1¾lb clams, washed

½ cup water
1 cup cherry tomatoes, halved
1 cup fish stock
3 Tbsp finely chopped parsley
salt and freshly ground black pepper
bruschetta to serve

method

1 Heat the oil in a large heavy-based saucepan and add the shallots, garlic, and chili. Cook for 1 minute and add the clams. Cover the pan and cook for 2 minutes, then add the water. Cook for a further 2 minutes, shaking the pan occasionally.

2 Add the cherry tomatoes, fish stock, and parsley and continue cooking for a further 5 minutes. If any clams are not open, tap with a spoon; if they still do not open, remove and discard. Season to taste and then serve in a large bowl with some bruschetta.

Creamy clam hot pot

Large clams are normally quite tough but cooked this way they are lovely and tender. If you are using smaller clams, reduce the cooking time or they will become tough.

SERVES: 4

Preparation time: 10 minutes plus
    2–3 hours soaking time
Cooking time: 15 minutes

4½lb large chowder clams
2 Tbsp olive oil
4 garlic cloves, finely chopped
4 shallots, finely chopped
1 cup heavy cream
salt and freshly ground black pepper
1 tsp finely chopped chives

method

1 Wash and scrub the clams and place in a large plastic container filled with water and add a good pinch of salt. Leave them for 2–3 hours to remove any sand or grit in the clams. Discard any clams that are open.

2 Heat the olive oil in a large pan, add the garlic and shallots, and cook for 30 seconds. Add the clams and, using a wooden spoon to stir and turn them, cook for 1 minute on each side. Add the cream, a pinch of salt, and some black pepper and cook for a further 10–15 minutes, or until all the clams are open—you may need to add a little water during this time.

3 Place the clams in a large bowl, discarding any that have not opened, and cover with the sauce. Sprinkle with the chives and serve immediately.

Right: Large American clam hot pot

1 It is best to use diver scallops if possible as dredged scallops can contain a lot of grit.

2 Grasp hold of the scallop and insert the knife between the two halves of the shell. Twist the knife slightly to make a wider gap.

3 Run the blade along the inner shell to cut through the ligament that joins the meat to the shell.

4 Open up the scallop and lift off the top half of the shell.

Diver scallops St Jacques

This is a very old recipe but none the less a very tasty one. The choice of cheese you use is entirely up to you, although I would stay away from really strong cheeses or you will lose the flavor of the scallops.

SERVES: 4

Preparation time: 10 minutes
Cooking time: 10 minutes

¾ cup dry white wine
1 bay leaf
4 peppercorns
1 onion, finely chopped
2 Tbsp butter
1½ Tbsp all-purpose flour
¾ cup milk
salt and freshly ground black pepper
¼ cup finely diced fontina cheese
1 tsp Dijon mustard
12 scallops on the ½ shell
2 Tbsp dry breadcrumbs
½ cup grated Parmesan cheese

method

1 Place the wine, bay leaf, peppercorns, and onion in a small pan and bring to a boil, then reduce the heat and simmer until the liquid has reduced by three quarters. Strain the liquid and set aside.

2 Melt the butter in a small pan and add the flour, cook for 1 minute, stirring continuously, then remove from the heat and gradually stir in the milk and the wine reduction, stirring until smooth. Return the pan to the heat and continue stirring until the mixture thickens. Season with salt and black pepper, then add the fontina cheese and the mustard.

3 Preheat the broiler. Spoon this mixture over the scallops and sprinkle with breadcrumbs and Parmesan. Cook under the broiler until crisp and golden brown and serve immediately.

5 Slide the knife under the scallop and remove any muscle.

6 Remove and discard the frilly orangey-gray intestine underneath the scallop and the black intestine, which runs along the side.

7 Trim the scallop and you should end up with a clean white scallop and a bright orange roe.

Scallop ceviche with chili, green onions, and soy

Scallops are a great shellfish to eat raw, but make sure they are absolutely fresh. You can use other scallops for this dish but divers work best as they tend not to have any grit or sand in them.

SERVES: 4

Preparation time: 15 minutes
plus 1 hour chilling time

12 fresh diver scallops, prepared
sea salt
juice of 1 lime
juice of ½ lemon
extra virgin olive oil
1 garlic clove, finely chopped
2 red chilies, seeded and finely
chopped
1 bunch cilantro, chopped
6 green onions, chopped
¼ cup soy sauce

method

1 Thinly slice the scallops and place them in a wide, flat-bottomed dish.

2 Sprinkle with sea salt, then pour over lime and lemon juice, cover with extra virgin olive oil, and then add the garlic, chili, cilantro, and green onions. Leave in the refrigerator for 1 hour. (The longer you leave it the more the flavors will be absorbed by the scallops.)

3 For presentation, place the thin slices of scallops on 4 clean dry scallop shells, drizzle with the soy sauce, and serve.

Pan-fried scallops

Scallops are one of those shellfish that eveyone loves. They are best cooked very simply and really don't need anything to add flavor to them as they have such an amazing taste of their own.

SERVES: 4

Preparation time: 10 minutes
Cooking time: 2 minutes

¼ cup balsamic vinegar
1 tsp sea salt
12 scallops, cleaned and roe
   removed
6 cups baby spinach leaves to serve

method

1 Heat the balsamic vinegar in a pan until reduced by half.

2 Place a grill pan on top of the stove and heat until very hot. Sprinkle the grill pan with the sea salt and sear the scallops for 1 minute on each side. (The salt prevents the scallops from sticking to the pan.)

3 Pile some baby spinach leaves in the center of each plate and surround with 3 scallops per portion. Pour the balsamic reduction on top of the spinach leaves.

PREPARING OYSTERS

1 You will need a special oyster knife in order to open oysters without cutting your hand open at the same time!

2 Push the knife through the small gap between the hinge, and twist until the hinge breaks.

3 Open the shell gently, using the knife to cut through any remaining muscle.

4 Slide the knife under the oyster and free it from the shell, taking care to retain the oyster juices.

Oyster tempura

If I am going to cook oysters, this is the way I prefer: nice and fluffy—lovely! You could also serve this dish with a sweet chili sauce—it makes a great snack before a dinner party.

SERVES: 4

Preparation time: 10 minutes
   plus 25 minutes resting time
   for batter
Cooking time: 4 minutes

2 cups rice flour
1 level tsp salt
1 egg, beaten
700ml bottle of sparkling water
24 rock oysters in ½ shell
vegetable oil for frying
2 limes, cut into wedges
½ cup soy sauce
1 Tbsp chopped cilantro

method

1 In a large bowl mix 1½ cups of the flour, the salt, and egg and then add the water a little at a time until the batter is smooth. Leave to cool in the refrigerator for 25 minutes.

2 Take the oysters out of the shell and coat them in the remaining flour, then dip them in the batter, making sure they are completely covered.

3 Heat the oil to about 340°F and fry the battered oysters for about 3–4 minutes until crispy. Serve with lime wedges, soy sauce, and chopped cilantro.

Oysters on ice with shallots, red wine vinegar, and lemon

Raw oysters are one of those shellfish that you either love or hate. If you have never eaten a raw oyster before, make sure that you squeeze lemon juice on it and watch to make sure it contracts before you eat it.

SERVES: 4

Preparation time: 10 minutes plus
   2 hours chilling time

salt
4 turns freshly ground black pepper
⅔ cup red wine vinegar
3 Tbsp good red wine
10 shallots, finely chopped
crushed ice to serve
24 native oysters
2 lemons, halved

method

1 Make the shallot dressing by combining ½ teaspoon of salt, pepper, vinegar, wine, and shallots in a bowl. Leave in the refrigerator for at least 2 hours.

2 Place some crushed ice on 4 serving plates and sprinkle with salt to prevent it melting too quickly. Make sure the oysters are freed from the shell, then place each on a half shell on top of the crushed ice. Serve with lemon halves and individual bowls of the shallot dressing.

Index

Page numbers preceded by the abbreviation (alt) denote the fish is listed as an alternative

Adriatic fish stew 130
American lobsters 111
Anchovy(ies) 66, (alt) 80, (alt) 82
   marinated 84

Baby smoked herring with beets and soured cream 90
Baked cod with black olive crust and lentils 21
Baked stuffed sardines 77
Baking in parchment 57
Barbecued red emperor with herb relish 106
Barbecued salmon with potato salad 74
Barbecued trout in newspaper 76
Barracuda (alt) 36, 94, (alt) 104
   shiitake teriyaki 106
Barramundi 94
   with shellfish, braised 104
Bay scallops 112
Black cod 12, (alt) 28
Black-shell mussels 112
Boneless herring dipped in egg and fried in garlic butter 82
Boning sardines, cleaning and 80
Bouillabaisse, sea robin 34
Braised barramundi with shellfish 105
Breading sole or other fish fillets 62
Bream 12, (alt) 13, (alt) 14, (alt) 32, (alt) 38, (alt) 95, (alt) 98
   stuffed with thyme and pan-fried in lemon oil 18
   red (alt) 96
   sea (alt) 100
Brill 48, (alt) 54, (alt) 62
   Mediterranean-style 49
Broiled langoustines 119
Butterfish (alt) 79, 94
   with tamarind and chili sauce 95
Butterflying jumbo shrimp 114

Cajun-style mackerel 68
Canadian lobsters 111
Carp 12
   poached in beer 31
Catfish 12, (alt) 31
   in cornmeal 36

Chinese squid 43
Chowder clam 112
Clam(s) 112, (alt) 132
   hot pot, creamy 134
   in their own juice 134
   with Asian herbs and noodles, razor 133
   see also Littleneck clams
Cleaning
   and boning sardines 80
   and filleting mackerel 68
   and filleting salmon 70
   and gutting round fish 14
   and scaling snapper 96
   see also Preparing
Coalfish *see* Pollock
Cod 12, (alt) 27, (alt) 31, (alt) 40, (alt) 58, (alt) 60, (alt) 63, (alt) 74, (alt) 104, (alt) 105
   with black olive crust and lentils, baked 21
   caldeirada, salt 38
   fish cakes with parsley sauce, salt 40
   fish pie 35
   in teriyaki and mango 28
Codling (alt) 27, (alt) 31, (alt) 63
Coley *see* Pollock
Common mussels 112
Crab(s) 110, (alt) 114, (alt) 121, (alt) 129
   and vegetable frittata 128
   claws pan fried with pesto 128
   Creole 127
   Dungeness 110, (alt) 129
   meat (alt) 40, (alt) 116
   preparing 126
   soft-shell 110
   spider 110
Crayfish 110
   salad with mango and citrus dressing 121
Creamy clam hot pot 134
Creole crab 127
Cuttlefish (alt) 43

Dab 48, (alt) 50
Diver scallops St Jacques 136
Dolphin fish *see* Mahi mahi
Dorado *see* Mahi mahi
Dover sole (alt) 24, 48, (alt) 50, (alt) 54
   fillets Dijon 52
   with peas and tomato sauce 50

Dublin Bay prawn *see* Langoustines
Dungeness crab 110, (alt) 129

Eel (alt) 31, 66
   endive, and radicchio salad, smoked 88
English sole 48, (alt) 50, (alt) 52, (alt) 63
   in parchment 57
   rolls stuffed with leeks, carrots, and shrimp 54
European lobsters 111

Filleting
   flat fish 52
   John Dory 22
   mackerel, cleaning and 68
   round fish 20
   salmon, cleaning and 70
Fish cakes with parsley sauce, salt cod 40
Fish pie 35
Fish stew, Adriatic 130
Flat fish (alt) 52
   skinning and filleting 52
   see also names of fish
Flounder 48, (alt) 50
   with grapes, golden raisins, and balsamic vinegar 58
Fried whitebait with paprika 82
Frying fish fillets 36

Gravlax, making 85
   green onion pancakes with 84
Grayling (alt) 13, (alt) 16, (alt) 18
Gray mullet (alt) 14, (alt) 32, (alt) 34, (alt) 100
Green onion pancakes with gravlax 84
Grilled squid with sweet chili sauce and arugula 45
Grilled red mullet with bay leaves 13
Gutting round fish 14

Haddock 12, (alt) 57, (alt) 84, (alt) 88
   and avocado mousse, smoked 42
   fish pie 35
   tahini baked 27
Halibut (alt) 21, 48, (alt) 52, (alt) 57, (alt) 71, (alt) 105
   with lemon, red onion, and cilantro 60

with saffron sauce and stewed leeks 58
Herring 66, (alt) 67, (alt) 77
   with beets and soured cream, baby smoked 90
   dipped in egg and fried in garlic butter, boneless 82

John Dory 12, (alt) 21, (alt) 27, (alt) 38, (alt) 62, (alt) 100
   filleting 22
   with tapenade, mash, and spinach 22
Jumbo shrimp (alt) 43, 111, (alt) 122, (alt) 124
   butterflying 114
   Portuguese style 115

Langoustine(s) 111, (alt) 115
   bisque 118
   broiled 119
   preparing 118
   with tomato sauce, fried 62
Littleneck clams 112, (alt) 133
Lobster(s) 111, (alt) 114, (alt) 118
   burgers with chili relish 124
   in Grand Marnier and kumquat sauce 124
   preparing 122
   thermidor 122

Mackerel (alt) 21, 66, (alt) 77, (alt) 82
   Cajun-style 68
   cleaning and filleting 68
   with mustard and lemon butter 67
   pâté, spicy 88
   smoked (alt) 91
Mahi mahi 94, (alt) 106
   poached in milk with herb sauce 102
Marinated anchovies 84
Marlin 94
   with black pepper and cream sauce 103
Mediterranean-style brill 49
Monkfish 12, (alt) 21, (alt) 31, (alt) 38, (alt) 58, (alt) 72, (alt) 78, (alt) 105, (alt) 106
   tails (alt) 16
   wrapped in Chinese cabbage, spiced 33
   wrapped in Parma ham 22

Mullet 12, (alt) 16, (alt) 18, (alt) 95,
    (alt) 106
    see also Grey mullet, Red mullet
Mussels 112
    diablo 131
    with herb breadcrumbs, au gratin
    132
    preparing 130

Native oyster 112
Norway lobsters *see* Langoustines

Octopus (alt) 45
Oyster(s) 112
    on ice with shallots, red wine
      vinegar, and lemon 141
    preparing 140
    tempura 140

Pan-fried English sole with tomato
    sauce 62
Pan-fried perch with béarnaise sauce
    21
Pan-fried scallops 139
Pan-frying whole fish 100
Parrot fish (alt) 16, (alt) 79, 94
    with red curry paste 98
Perch 12
    with béarnaise sauce, pan-fried 21
Pilchards *see* Sardines
Plaice 48, (alt) 49, (alt) 50, (alt) 52,
    (alt) 54, (alt) 62
    goujons in sparkling wine batter 63
Poaching 31
Pollock 12, (alt) 27
    sour orange 31
Pomfret *see* Butterfish
Potted shrimp 116
Preparing
    crab 126
    langoustine 118
    lobster 122
    mussels 130
    oysters 140
    scallops 136
    squid 44
    see also Cleaning

Rainbow trout (alt) 74
Razor clam(s) 112
    with Asian herbs and noodles 133
Red bream (alt) 96

Red emperor 94
    with herb relish, barbecued 106
Red mullet with bay leaves, grilled
    13
Red snapper 12, (alt) 14, (alt) 68, (alt)
    96
    sesame baked 16
Rock oyster 112
Rosemary tuna kabobs 78

Saithe *see* Pollock
Salmon (alt) 18, (alt) 21, (alt) 40, (alt)
    42, (alt) 58, (alt) 61, 66, (alt) 68,
    (alt) 74, (alt) 76, (alt) 86, (alt) 102,
    (alt) 105
    with bok choy and soy sauce 73
    carpaccio with pine nuts and soy
      sauce 87
    cleaning and filleting 70
    parcel 71
    with potato salad, barbecued 74
    slicing 87
    smoked (alt) 84
    steaks, cutting 74
    stuffed with crab and spinach with
      dill sauce 71
Salmon trout (alt) 71
Salt cod
    caldeirada 38
    fish cakes with parsley sauce 40
Sardines 66, (alt) 67, (alt) 82, (alt) 88
    baby (alt) 84
    baked stuffed 77
    cleaning and boning 80
    with spaghetti Sicilian style 80
    smoked (alt) 90
Sashimi of sea bass 42
Scaling snapper, cleaning and 96
Scallop(s) (alt) 57, (alt) 78, (alt) 87,
    112, (alt) 115, (alt) 119, (alt) 128
    ceviche with ginger, chili, green
      onions, and soy 138
    pan-fried 139
    preparing 136
    St Jacques, diver 136
Scottish lobsters 111
Sea bass 12, (alt) 18, (alt) 28, (alt) 33,
    (alt) 58, (alt) 60, (alt) 61, (alt) 73,
    (alt) 76, (alt) 86, (alt) 98
    sashimi of 42
    Thai roast 14
    with Thai herbs, steamed 32

Sea bream (alt) 34, (alt) 100
Sea robin 12
    bouillabaisse 34
Sea scallops 112
Sea trout and noodle salad 74
Seafood risotto 120
Seared tuna with sticky rice, wasabi,
    and soy sauce 86
Sesame baked red snapper 16
Shad 12
    stuffed with sorrel and served with
      beurre blanc 18
Shark (alt) 36, 94
    steaks Moroccan style 105
Shrimp 111, (alt) 118, (alt) 119, (alt)
    121, (alt) 128
    with brandy pâté 116
    butterflying jumbo 114
    curry, Thai 113
    Portuguese style, jumbo 113
    potted 116
    soufflé 114
    see also Jumbo shrimp
Skate (alt) 22, 48
    with black butter 50
Skinning
    and filleting flat fish 52
    salt cod 38
Slicing salmon 87
Smoked eel, endive, and raddichio
    salad 88
Smoked haddock and avocado
    mousse 42
Smoked herring with beets and
    soured cream, baby 90
Smoked mackerel (alt) 91
Smoked salmon (alt) 84
Smoked sardines (alt) 90
Smoked trout (alt) 88
    and potato salad 91
Snapper (alt) 13, (alt) 16, (alt) 22,
    (alt) 76, (alt) 105, (alt) 106
    cleaning and scaling 96
    see also Red snapper, Yellowtail
      snapper
Soft-shell crab 110
Sole (alt) 49
    breading 62
    see also Dover sole, English sole
Sour orange pollock 31
Spiced monkfish wrapped in Chinese
    cabbage 33

Spicy baked yellowtail snapper with
    pine nuts 96
Spicy mackerel pâté 88
Spider crab 110
    with linguine and zucchini 129
Sprats (alt) 82, (alt) 84
Squid 12, (alt) 45
    Chinese 43
    preparing 44
    with sweet chili sauce and arugula,
      grilled 45
Steamed sea bass with Thai herbs 32
Stuffing a whole fish 19
Swordfish (alt) 33, (alt) 36, (alt) 61,
    66, (alt) 74, (alt) 78, (alt) 86, (alt)
    87, (alt) 103, (alt) 105
    paillard on Caesar salad 72

Tahini baked haddock 27
Thai shrimp curry 113
Thai roast sea bass 14
Tilapia 94
    with fruit sauce 100
Trout (alt) 31, 66, (alt) 73, (alt) 77
    with apples, cider, and cream 79
    and noodle salad, sea 74
    and potato salad, smoked 91
    rainbow trout (alt) 74
    smoked (alt) 88
    wrapped in newspaper 76
    see also Salmon trout
Tuna (alt) 21, (alt) 33, (alt) 36, (alt) 42,
    66, (alt) 68, (alt) 72, (alt) 74, (alt)
    87, (alt) 103
    kabobs, rosemary 78
    with sticky rice, wasabi, and soy
      sauce, seared 86
Turbot (alt) 24, 48, (alt) 58, (alt) 60,
    (alt) 71
    hollandaise 61

Whelks 112
Whitebait 66
    with paprika, fried 82
Wrapping fish fillets in Parma ham 24

Yellowtail snapper 94
    with pine nuts, spicy baked 96

Acknowledgments

First and foremost, thank you to all of you who have bought this book. I hope you enjoy it as much as I enjoyed writing it. Nevertheless, if it wasn't for my publisher, Jacqui Small, getting together with my agent, Fiona Lindsey, this would never have happened, so thanks to you both.

A huge thanks to my wife, Nikki, for putting up with my weekends working in my office at home, working on holidays, and even on the plane!

Thanks to my long-lasting PA, Luisa, for working wonders with all my scribbles and testing the recipes, so now she can apply for a home economist job!

And thanks to David Munns for being the most patient photographer I have ever met!

Big thanks to all at Billingsgate Fish Market and Borough Market for all their help.